"I love good stories, and these are among the very best. Kim Meeder writes with a mesmerizing, wonderfully refreshing beauty. If your soul needs a fresh touch, reading this book is like opening a door and welcoming hope inside."

ALICE GRAY,
BESTSELLING COMPILER OF *Stories for the Heart*

"Wonderful...Exhilarating...Inspirational.... Kim Meeder captures that special bond between humans and horses, telling us why it's the little things that make each day worth living."

BEN WESTLUND,
OREGON STATE REPRESENTATIVE

"*Hope Rising* details the amazing accounts from a special ranch that I have been privileged to support. These memorable stories will touch you deeply."

BEV CLARNO,
OREGON STATE SENATOR

Hope Rising

KIM MEEDER

God Bless,

K

Multnomah Books

HOPE RISING
published by Multnomah Books

© 2003 by Kim Meeder
International Standard Book Number: 978-1-59052-269-1

Cover image by Lisa Kimmel/Photonica

Published in the United States by WaterBrook Multnomah, an imprint of the
Crown Publishing Group, a division of Random House Inc., New York.

MULTNOMAH and its mountain colophon are registered trademarks
of Random House Inc.

Printed in the United States of America

For information:
MULTNOMAH BOOKS
12265 ORACLE BOULEVARD, SUITE 200
COLORADO SPRINGS, CO 80921

Library of Congress Cataloging-in-Publication Data

Meeder, Kim.
Hope rising / by Kim Meeder.
p. cm.
ISBN 1-59052-269-9 (pbk.)
1. Crystal Peaks Youth Ranch (Bend, Or.) 2. Problem youth—Services
for—Oregon. 3. Horses—Therapeutic use. 4. Animal rescue—Oregon.
I. Title.

HV1435.O7M44 2003
362.7—dc21

2003006576

10—15 14 13

*This book is dedicated to Beth Everest,
my precious little grandma who bought my first horse for me.
Mimi! Look what you started!*

KIM MEEDER

2004 Recipient of the
Jacqueline Kennedy Onassis Award for Public Service

In 1972, Jacqueline Kennedy Onassis, U.S. Senator Robert Taft Jr., and Sam Beard founded the American Institute for Public Service, a 501c3 public foundation to establish a Nobel Prize for public and community service -- The Jefferson Awards.

The Jefferson Awards are presented on two levels: national and local. National award recipients represent a "Who's Who" of outstanding Americans. On the local level, Jefferson Award recipients are ordinary people who do extraordinary things without expectation of recognition or reward.

Kim Meeder was honored at the Jefferson Awards National Celebration of Service to America in Washington, D.C. on June 29, 2004. She was one of four regional recipients of the Jefferson Award and one of five national recipients to receive the Jacqueline Kennedy Onassis Award for greatest public service benefiting the local community. Soon after, she received a Red Cross Local Heroes Award which was read before Congress. Crystal Peaks Youth Ranch has since been blessed with visitors from around the world who not only seek healing for themselves, but also wish to give of themselves for the sake of helping others.

The Place Where Hope Rises

Sometimes it is only through devastation that we find the truth. Hardship can be like a savage cleansing fire. All the things we think of as necessary to our survival are soon revealed as nothing more than the dross of complacent luxury, consumed by the fire as it burns down to the true metal of the soul. Hardship uncovers the only thing we truly need to survive—hope.

Within every heart there exists a special place, a place where the hopes and dreams of the soul soar, unchained by logical or physical entrapments. For some, visiting this unique place is a frivolous waste of time, a mental blowing of dandelion spores.

For others this place becomes the mountain meadow within their soul, the sweeping expanse of wildflowers and fragrant grasses, the streams of pure glacial water, where the spirit runs free.

It is a place where the impossible flourishes, where dreams survive the inferno of reality to become the miraculous wonders that draw us forward—it is the place where hope rises.

* All of the stories in *Hope Rising* are true. Some of the names have been changed to protect the privacy of the people involved.

Table of Contents

My Gratitude for Hope Shared

How can one thank every grain of sand on the beach or every twinkling star in the heavens? All the tender souls who have graced this work, have, in their own unique way, added richness to my life. I am intensely grateful for each one.

I am thankful for...

My husband, Troy

Your constant love and support have made this ministry possible.
Without you my heart, my soul, and my life would be incomplete.

Ami Johnston

Your dedication to this project has been
as unwavering as the mountain skyline.
Without you I would have nothing but
a binder full of handwritten pages.

Judy Gordon and Margaret Sharpe

Your miraculous efforts have guided this book
through the exhausting editing process.
Without both of you I would have no mirror.

Sue Morgan

You are one of my broadest shoulders.
Without you my heart would be missing the joy of
sharing the high wilderness places.

My Lord

Above all, my gratitude goes to You and
Your sacrifice of love made for me, so that I could live.
Without You, I would have no love, no light, no breath…no hope.

To My Ranch Kids

You're my handful of flowers,
   My skippin' rocks on the creek,
My melted ice cream,
   Sweet kisses on my cheek.

You're my shining light,
   My little twinkling star,
The bounce in my step,
   My last cookie in the jar.

You're the miracle of life,
   You're the joy of first birth;
And all because of you
   I'm the richest girl on earth.

Kim Meeder

hope

rising

from

stone

Angels in Horsehair

ADAM WAS SO SMALL for his age. It was the first thing I noticed when his caseworker introduced us. His eyes, shadowed with sadness, were too large for his little face. He was drawn into himself, as if he were trying to fit his diminutive frame into an even smaller space. It was clear that this child had known more terror in his handful of years than most knew in a lifetime.

The pair had traveled to the ranch unannounced with the hope of simply petting the soft muzzles of my "angels in horsehair." Even though the ranch was alive with children, Adam stood apart, completely alone—a tiny brown-eyed lamb lost in his own skin.

I smiled at him. He immediately looked to the ground in retreat. My heart staggered under the weight of his loneliness. I prayed that God would meet this child in this place in a special way.

I knelt down and quietly tried to engage Adam in a simple conversation. I asked him if he had ever ridden a horse before. He stared at the ground, somber as an ancient sage, and silently shook his head. "Would you like to?" I asked. His little head snapped up, and he looked me directly in the eyes with more than a little disbelief. I smiled into his questioning face. "We have a pony for you," I told him. "A very special pony who would very much like to meet you."

"Really?" he asked, with more emotion than I'm sure anyone had seen in a while. He looked at his caseworker and then back at me. I told him where the halters were and pointed back behind the arena to where the golden pony, Hobbs, lived. Adam flashed us a little grin and took off at a run.

From a distance, in that moment he must have looked like every other child at the ranch. But from my view, I was horrified! His grin revealed a mouth full of broken teeth. He ran on ahead of us. I could feel my neck prickle before I turned to his counselor and quietly asked, "Is that what I think it is?"

It took her a long moment to answer. When she did, her voice was choked by the grip of anger and compassion. "It's so much worse than you could imagine," she finally stated. "A father is supposed to love, cherish, and protect his son. Not only has Adam's 'dad' broken most of his son's teeth with his fists, but before he went to prison, he would get drunk and make his son run around the yard while he shot at him with a rifle!"

We walked on in silence. Both of us watched Adam enter the pony's paddock and begin stroking his face. "It's a miracle he's still alive," she finally said.

Together, Adam and I led the pony back to the hitching post and went through the grooming and tacking process. Often I placed my hands over his to guide them. I held Hobbs's hooves and Adam cleaned them. I lifted the saddle into place, and he cinched up the girth. Then it was time to put on the bridle. I showed the little boy where his hands and fingers should be, how to hold his arms, and where he should stand. Then I placed his hands so that they gripped the bridle in the right way, and gently moved him toward the pony's left shoulder. It was up to him now. Silently I stepped back and watched.

Adam stood quietly for a moment, as if taking in all that he had just learned. And suddenly, Hobbs did something I have never seen any horse do before or since. As the child stood by the pony's shoulder, Hobbs reached around with his head and neck and pressed Adam into his body. The pony held him so tightly in the curve of his neck that he could not raise his arms.

For long moments the pony stayed that way, encircling Adam's tiny body with his neck. He couldn't move anything except his eyes. They rolled back to look at me. I could clearly see that Adam was afraid.

What was Hobbs doing? I could think of only one thing to say. The words all came out in a rush. "Oh, my gosh! I think that this pony is giving you a hug!"

Adam's huge, startled eyes moved in pinball fashion as he tried to process what was happening.

"I have never seen him do that to anyone else," I added. "You must be very special."

Adam's face began to relax with my reassurance. He appeared to accept what I'd said. Slowly he wriggled his right arm out and began to hug the pony back. For a brief moment, this battered child was allowed to be nothing more than a little boy who was loved by a pony. Adam's head slowly dropped until it rested against Hobbs's neck. Like a whispered prayer, more to himself than to anyone else, he began saying over and over, "He likes me...he likes me...he likes me."

It was several minutes before Hobbs relaxed his grip on the child. Adam, seemingly so overwhelmed that anything on this earth would choose to love him, clung tightly to the pony with both arms, pressing his face into Hobbs's golden body.

Moments passed and the boy's hug melted into long strokes on both sides of the pony's neck. The stony tomb that had once imprisoned Adam's heart began to crumble under newfound love. Finally, he looked up and smiled. It was a radiant, jagged grin, so dazzling it was like trying to look at the sun. With his arms still around the pony, he turned and looked up at me. "He likes me!" he said again. But this time he said it out loud, with a convincing sparkle in his eyes.

I glanced toward heaven with a wink and a smile and whispered, "Thank You."

Eli's Whirlwind

WHIRLWINDS ARE a common occurrence in this place we now call our home. They come in every shape and size. Most of the time they are harmless, but Troy and I were shocked when we first saw them snatch up several wind shelters—each weighing more than a ton—lift them off their foundations and hurl them through the air. We've seen fifty-gallon drums flung over two hundred feet. We've watched as piles of information sheets, release waivers, and children's drawings of horses were swept heavenward in a spiraling vertical stampede.

Most of the whirlwinds are small enough to be nothing more than playful sprites, beckoning children to run and catch them. Forsaking the task at hand and unmindful of ears full of grit, kids will dash into the spinning dust devils, squealing with laughter as their hair is snatched straight upward in the vortex.

Although they are a bit tumultuous at times, I find the whirlwinds a source of enormous beauty, intrigue, and—perhaps paradoxically—of comfort. They are a visual encapsulation of something invisible. We cannot see the wind; we can only see the evidence of it.

No matter when a whirlwind occurs, I can't help but stop what I'm doing to stand and watch in awe. Like the fleeting glimpse of a shooting star or a bolt of lightning, whirlwinds are a rare and wonderful sight meant only for those chosen few who turn their heads and open their eyes. They fill my heart with an intensely personal confirmation that my Lord is near.

It was Monday morning, and calls came in like a wild train of roller-coaster cars careening out of control—outraged callers burning with angry fire, concerned people pleading for merciful intercession in a case of neglect, officials looking for answers to the legal questions. One thing was clear: A horse was in desperate need.

When Troy and I began our equine rescue operation at Crystal Peaks, we had no idea how much the area needed such a place. Even before we obtained our nonprofit status, the calls for help came in like a flood.

Several came from distraught owners who had entrusted a horse to a trainer, only to have their equine friend returned to them untouchable after being brutally beaten or mishandled. Some calls came from owners who no longer wanted the bother of caring for an injured horse. For me, that was the worst. These horses had given everything they had through the best years of their lives— carrying their owners to remarkable victories, growing up with their children, creating lifetimes of adventure and joy. These faithful companions had poured their hearts and strength into their families, and now, broken beyond apparent usefulness or recovery, they were unwanted and cast aside. Many were from concerned neighbors who couldn't stand to see a horse being abused or neglected any longer. Such was the case of this whirlwind of calls.

Armed only with this urgent tornado of information, I drove our old truck to the address given. Pulling off to the side of the crumbling, twisted road, I turned off the ignition and for a moment simply stared. None of the calls had led me to expect what I saw. Even from a hundred yards away, it was hideously clear that this horse needed immediate, intensive care.

Fighting back a wave of self-conscious intimidation, I made my way silently down the long paved drive. I was not a guest in this place but an intercessor, an intruder who might become the target of vicious, hurling accusations. It would have been easy to turn and run. No one would ever know of my flinching cowardice—no one except maybe the hollow-eyed skeleton of a horse whose very existence begged for my compassion.

My reluctant passage toward the rising monolith of a house seemed to stretch out before me like a never-ending journey. My steps were quick and conspicuously quiet as I made my way to the main entrance.

With each step I felt the growing weight of impending confrontation. I hated this part of any rescue operation—the feeling that I am about to awaken some slumbering disaster that lurks just beyond my sight.

The house loomed above me. It was neat and tidy and showed obvious pride of ownership. The sound of my hesitant knocking against the wood-framed door seemed to blow away in the gentle afternoon breeze. No one answered. No one home, I presumed—probably too readily.

I retreated down the walk and followed the path that led down the slope to the barn. I had to know. I had to see for myself.

I felt rather than heard the groan that escaped my lips

as the horse's horrific condition came into closer view. He was too weak even to acknowledge my presence. His jagged spine jutted three inches above his sunken ribcage. His hip bones protruded so sharply that they threatened to burst through his shriveled hide. His eyes reflected nothing. All his remaining strength was somberly focused inward, on the mere task of staying alive.

The ragged remains of his winter coat, which once must have been a rich caramel color, did little to maintain his sparse body heat. An obviously extended bout of diarrhea had left open sores over most of his rump and hind legs. Closer examination revealed that he was so emaciated that his rectum had receded within his body more than five inches. The abnormal tunnel that now exited his body was horizontal, so that his own runny waste had collected there. This grotesque buildup was literally rotting an infected hole into his ravaged body.

Anger and sorrow twisted violently together within me. A storm of emotion gripped my throat until I felt like I was choking. Caught somewhere between shouting and screaming, raging and crying, I began, instead, to run. I raced past the immaculate house and back down the long paved drive, trying to outrun my fury. Confrontation can become a monster that I prefer to avoid. But this time the monster was swept away by the ferocity of my outrage.

A flurry of telephone calls followed my visit. The necessary information was exchanged, the paperwork completed. And at last Troy and I repeated my earlier trip down the cracked and twisted highway—this time pulling our trailer behind us.

I spoke quietly with the owners when we arrived. They appeared pleasant and kind. Their deadly flaw, it seemed, was a crippling lack of observation. With my sunglasses in place, I watched over their shoulders as Troy gently guided our new charge toward the empty trailer. Their polite words fell short between us as my attention was focused on the ravaged gelding.

Every step was so hard for him. But, amazingly, when he saw the open trailer, his head rose slightly, and he reached more with his legs to close the distance. He knew. With an enormous display of pure will, he gathered his remaining weight, and with one great effort lunged off his hind legs into the horse trailer. He was like the survivor of a shipwreck, giving all he had to leap into a waiting lifeboat. Afterward he stood motionless in the trailer, gasping from the exertion of lifting his own weight fourteen inches off the ground.

Back at the ranch, we carefully unloaded him in the common area and began the excruciatingly long journey—seventy-five yards—from there to his recovery paddock. Twice we had to stop and rest as he swayed with utter exhaustion. "You're going to be okay, big boy," we coaxed him. "Everything is going to be all right. Just a few more steps...you're almost home." I stroked his neck and reassured him constantly as we waited for him to catch his breath.

The sun had already slipped below the serrated horizon. Long shadows melted into inky pools that silently converged in a rising wave of twilight. I glanced at Troy over the gelding's sagging neck and saw my grief mirrored in his face. We had no words, but our unspoken communication was enough—in such a moment, what truly can be said?

Two and a half days passed, and I felt growing concern

for our sweet gelding. Physically he was progressing, thanks to good nutrition and medical care. But his attitude was still inward and depressed. He had not yet acknowledged my presence or anyone else's.

I studied him through the fence, thinking, *Somewhere I'm missing the mark. I'm not getting through to him.* He seemed mentally trapped in a downward spiral, still under the weight of imminent death that had threatened him for so long. Even with that threat removed, he had given up hope. His light was going out.

Suddenly, I couldn't stand to watch this sickening process any longer. I realized that, despite all we had done, this horse was going to die.

I wanted him to know that he was cherished. With measured deliberation, I led him back down to the hitching post. After tying him off, I put together a special tray of all our finest grooming aids. He deserved the best we had. In silence, I massaged a special mix of oil and fragrance into the hair of his black mane. Working carefully, I separated each strand until the once matted and tangled web lay smooth and flat, glistening under the warm rays of the afternoon sun. Then I did the same with his tail.

After that I began brushing his body. His ragged buckskin coat literally peeled back like a rotten carpet. Overwhelming sadness filled my eyes with tears. Instead of revealing a glossy summer coat underneath, his skin was all but naked. The total neglect he had suffered had robbed his body of the ability to grow normal body hair. His black skin was barely supporting the first signs of a golden layer of peach fuzz. Mechanically my arms continued to brush. I wept out loud.

The warm air hung in stillness. Sparrows in a nesting

box overhead sang over their newly hatched family. Horsehair covered the ground in a four-inch layer of gold around my feet. I brushed and cried as our gelding's hideous body was fully unveiled. Finally I leaned against him with both hands on his shoulder and began to pray. From above angels saw a filthy woman bowing over a skeletal horse on a cloud of golden hair.

Time slipped by. Then very subtly I felt the horse's weight shift. I looked up to see his large, black nostrils close to my face. He had curved his neck around as far as he could, and for the first time he was looking at me! I held his gaze. It was still sunken, but the unmistakable twinkle of life had triumphantly returned to his once dulled eyes.

I stepped toward his outstretched muzzle and, with both arms, cradled his head against my chest. The spiral of death had stopped, and by the breath of a merciful God had been blown back in the reverse direction. I knew in that moment, he had chosen to live. Gently we held our embrace, my wet cheek pressed against his forehead.

I was lifting my head to kiss his face when I saw it. It was about ten feet wide and rotating slowly across the yard. The whirlwind, with unhurried deliberation, moved toward us until we were completely enveloped. The entire mass of cottony hair rose up around us in a golden column, slowly spiraling up into heaven.

Cradling the gelding's head, I watched in breathless awe as nearly every wisp of his fallen hair lazily rotated upward and gradually out of sight.

Still gazing skyward, I knew that my simple prayer had been answered. Like Elijah, the faithful Old Testament prophet who was drawn into heaven by a whirlwind so that he might not experience death, so this equine friend had his hair drawn into the good Lord's domain. It was a symbolic answer to my prayer, as clear to my heart as a booming voice from the sky. I knew that this horse, "Eli" as I immediately christened him, would not die then or anytime soon.

And the answer had been sent to me in a package that I would immediately recognize. For all heaven knows that the sight of a whirlwind fills my heart with an intensely personal confirmation that my Lord is near.

Metamorphosis

❧

I STOOD ON TOP of the hill, looking down on all that I was soon to own, and felt as though I were part of a surrealist painting. If I looked straight out, my heart and eyes could barely contain the sweeping, uninterrupted view of the majestic mountains that carry the skyline of Central Oregon. Lifting toward heaven, they rose before me like glistening, snow-covered teeth in a yawning canine jaw, soaring above valley and crevasse, towering ridge and rocky bluff. High above me, billowing clouds cast a leopardlike pattern of light and dark spots that moved across the undulating green canvas far below. It was massive. It would never be changed or obstructed by feeble manmade attempts to tame the horizon. It filled my heart.

I took a deep breath and placed my hands on my hips, trying to summon enough courage to look down. Directly below me and for several acres beyond, lay the obvious reason that my husband, Troy, and I were able to afford such spectacular property—we had just purchased our very own cinder pit.

Sprawling in all its cavernous glory, it looked as though a greedy giant had taken a monstrous three-acre bite out of the earth, leaving behind a gaping, red encrusted hole. All of the power and promise that the land had previously supported was gone. What had once been a beautiful butte now stood desolate, lifeless, broken beyond hope of repair. All of its intrinsic gifts had been razed away. The property was so hideous that many of our family and friends looked at it and turned away in disgust. Several laughed at our foolhardiness for ever wanting something so useless.

Although the land was completely destroyed, Troy and I saw something else. We didn't focus on what was, but what could be. With the help of local ranchers, we began to bury the cinder pit floor under organic waste materials—manure, straw, wood shavings—to build up a foundation that could again support life.

Troy, being a landscaper, brought home every bruised, broken, and unwanted tree; and together we planted them, digging holes through the floor of sheer rock. After hundreds of pick, bar, and shovel hours, and nearly as many blisters, our cinder pit was transformed into a remarkably functional and beautiful ranch.

It had become the perfect match. Broken property planted with more than three hundred broken trees and shrubs, filled with a herd of broken horses—all to love back to life thousands of broken children.

What once needed healing now gives healing. What was once broken has now been restored. What was once lost is now found.

Solo Flight

ｼｼ

ＴＯＤＡＹ ＷＡＳ ＴＨＥ day! With all
the moxie his nine-year-old heart could muster, Eric had
decided it was time to canter. With his helmet firmly
strapped in place and giving a little hike to his jeans, he
climbed to the center of the mounting block. Pure determination drew his small dark brows together as he
prepared to mount.

Once in the saddle, he reviewed his checklist with all
the focus of a fighter pilot. Through his little glasses, his
intense expression took in every detail of my coaching.
After a proper warm-up and many trotting drills, he was
ready. His little Adam's apple dipped with a hard swallow
as I gave him his final instructions. His piercing gaze left
me and focused down the arena rail in a symbolic gesture
that said, "There's no turning back."

I told him to trot an entire lap before giving his horse
the verbal and physical cues to canter. With a squaring of
his small shoulders and a proud lift of his little chin, he
set off with the seriousness of a soldier going to war.

His trotting lap was perfect, punctuated neatly by his
crisp posting in the saddle seat. His phantom marker to
canter was coming up...it was time. When he crossed the
imaginary line, his horse took flight with a small leap for-

ward. Eric's physical response was remarkably similar to someone who had just been shot out of a cannon! His head whipped back and his hands and feet flew up, flailing in every direction in a desperate attempt to regain his balance. In his head I'm certain that he was hearing the buzzing red-letter warning: EJECT!...EJECT!

The world spun past, but like a highly trained pilot, Eric didn't panic. One system at a time, he fixed each problem until his horse came to a full and complete stop.

"Yee haw, Cowboy!" I clapped and laughed as I went up to congratulate him. "Way to go, Eric. You did great!"

His little chest released a huge breath that was quickly followed by a nervous giggle. "Whew!" he sighed loudly. "That was really *hard*. Because both of my feet came out of the holsters!"

The Beginning

JESSICA NEVER spoke. Her heart, like the ancient city of Jericho, was tightly sealed in by immense walls of stone. In a spiraling chain reaction, she had lost everything a child depends on—attentive parents, a supportive family, a secure home. Now the shining dreams that every teen should have for the future had been shattered, far beyond despair—beyond, it seemed, any hope of rescue. Those destroyed hopes lay in the barren fortress of her heart—a maze of jagged shards scattered around her feet. She didn't dare take a step in any direction, not wishing to risk further injury by stepping on any of the splintered fragments of what used to be her life. Instead, as if standing in a minefield, she drew everything inside herself. Body, mind, soul, and spirit were gathered to form fragile, concentric circles until finally, a wounded phantom cowered in the center.

Only sixteen, Jessica's near albino coloring was too weak to cover the signs of stress that darkened the pale skin around her hollow eyes. Her slightly downturned lips were almost transparent, colored by the lightest shade of pale rose. Yet even under her tousle of blond hair, she was still sadly beautiful.

At first I was never certain why Jessica came to the ranch. Troy and I had just bought the property; we had no barn, no shelter, no tack room, no tack. Nothing but a corral, a hitching post—and two horses we had just rescued from starvation and abuse. We were working feverishly to build the most basic necessities to sustain them.

The horses were Jessica's excuse for making the long trip out to the ranch, and she came as often as she could afford the gas. Each time, as she climbed out of her battered car, her deep cobalt blue eyes briefly found mine. They were all that revealed the life still struggling to communicate from within the prison of her silence. Her gaze rose and fell as she attempted to balance her terror of rejection with pleading for acceptance. I was reminded of the trembling fear of a neglected puppy—needing so desperately to be cuddled, but too fearful to ask. I wanted nothing more than to scoop her into my arms, to hold her next to my heart, until she knew that she had found a haven where she could rest.

Initially, I thought that I needed to fill the long silences between us with words. It was exhausting, trying to carry on a one-sided conversation. But over time a wordless revelation crept into my brain. Jessica didn't come to listen to my endless chatter. She came for two simple reasons—she needed to feel safe, and she needed to feel loved. Neither took many words at all.

The horses we had rescued were still far too weak and starved even to carry a rider. Jessica didn't have much to offer either, but she gave all she had. At last her voiceless existence had begun to have a purpose outside herself. In each of our horses she had found another living creature—

also neglected and lonely—who needed her help to get well.

Watching them together was my first experience witnessing a child's attempts to make an animal better. I saw Jessica's confidence and sense of self-worth grow as she began to give, and receive back, unconditional love.

Jessica was a silent paradox. If I gazed at her a little too long, her large eyes fell like shattered stars, and I had the impression that the stress felt like a laser beam on her impoverished soul—that she might burn to ashes before my eyes and blow away. Yet she could wield a hammer for hours with all the strength of a man. Wordlessly, through those early days and weeks, she labored with us to build the foundations of what would one day become our ranch.

Looming large among the first of our jobs was the need for endless serpentine stretches of fencing all around the new property. Since the floor of the cinder pit was too rocky for digging, we soon gave up the idea of drilling postholes or driving stakes. Montana fencing seemed to be our only option—lodgepole A-frames ingeniously constructed to stand on top of the ground. The obvious drawback to this kind of fence is that hundreds of lodgepoles need to be measured, sawn, drilled, and then assembled with hardware to make the frames. They are awkward to handle and heavy to carry. Each frame has to be shouldered into position—one every ten feet—and then connected to the next by three twelve-foot poles. As interminable and exhausting as this process was, Jessica never appeared to tire of it. Nothing defeated her until the setting sun finally made it too dark to carry on.

One Wednesday a collision of moisture and bitter wind engulfed us in driving sleet. Usually the sight of the mountains sweeping upward from the ranch makes my heart soar, no matter how hard the work or what is going on in my life. This day they were shrouded behind an ominous blanket of gray.

After shouldering logs and poles into position for most of the morning, the tedious job of actually constructing the fence came almost as a welcome relief. Armed with power drills, twenty-five pounds of eight-inch lag screws, hundreds of washers, a hammer and a handsaw, Jessica and I slogged back up the storm-battered hillside.

The biting wind whipped stinging pellets into our faces as we worked. Icy trickles streamed down Jessica's flushed cheeks. Tendrils of hair had escaped her ponytail and were frozen to her coat, her neck, her lips. She didn't appear to notice but carried on with a bleak sort of strength.

When the heavy-duty drill batteries finally gave out, I thought we should take the thirty minutes needed to recharge them and recharge ourselves. We both needed to warm up and dry out, and I had a long-distance phone call to return. "Let's go up to the house," I said, "and have some tea."

Silently, Jessica shook her head. I implored her to come out of the storm and rest for a while, but she steadfastly refused. "I have to make this call," I told her. "Promise me, if you get too cold, that you'll come in." I was pleading by that time, but had to be satisfied with the almost imperceptible nod she gave me.

Indoors, the driving sleet sounded like glass beads spattering against the wall of windows that make up the front of our house. I turned on the lights and felt again the warm pleasure I always get when coming into my home. We've painted some of the walls to look like old parchment; others glow with a warm adobe red that makes just the right backdrop to our eclectic mix of western-style furniture and priceless yard-sale treasures. I shucked off my soaking coat in the welcome heat and put the kettle on to boil.

From inside, the storm looked worse, and I felt a pang as I saw in the distance Jessica's wraithlike form through the lashing sleet. I made the call, and what started as a quick few words stretched into a rich half-hour conversation. With an eye on the clock and thinking of Jessica, I wound up the call just as a movement outside caught my eye.

I stepped close to one of our big windows, and I saw that Jessica had led out our most recently rescued horse to the hitching post—a gray filly who was so impoverished when we found her that I was afraid she would have permanent leg damage. Although much improved from when we'd brought her to the ranch a few weeks ago, she was still emaciated and weak. Jessica had perched herself precariously on the post of the hitching rail, while she and the filly huddled their heads together, nose to nose. Intrigued, I pressed my face against the window. My breath fogged the glass, and absently I rubbed it clear. *Lord, what's going on?* I wondered.

Suddenly, Jessica lifted her head and sat upright. As if in some mysterious accord the filly's head bobbed up as well. Now I could see clearly what was happening. Liquid warmth flooded my eyes as in the silence of the house I realized exactly what they were doing. Jessica was talking! She began to add emphasis with her hands and arms.

Words bottled up for years—words that needed to be said—
were pouring out of her like a flood. The stone walls
around her heart, like those massive walls of Jericho in
ancient times, came tumbling down. With an angel's view I
watched Jessica speak, a vivid one-way conversation punctuated with waving hands and lifted eyebrows. From a
starving horse to a starving girl and back again, a torrent
of love washed away their barren places.

The driving sleet outside became a healing rain as a
destitute horse was allowed to go where no adult had been
in years—stepping through the minefield of Jessica's soul
to reach a broken child, in a flow of trust and love that
only God can truly understand.

At that instant I purposed in my heart to build the
kind of place where this miracle might happen over and
over again. A simple place where angels disguised as starving horses could reach out to the hearts and souls of
starving kids. It was a perfect match, forged in heaven
itself. It was the moment when Crystal Peaks Youth Ranch
was born.

What appeared that day to be the destruction of a
stony prison, the release of a tender, captive soul—the end
of a silent world—was really just the beginning.

hope
rising
within a
child's heart

The Wishing Tree

"Mama, THE WISHING Tree burned down!" Breanna cried, her voice as thin and small as her nine-year-old body. "I went with Heather to see if it was okay. But it wasn't. It burned down in the fire last week."

"Honey, I know about the fire," her mother said. "But what is this 'Wishing Tree'?"

The child took a deep breath, as if she needed fortification for the precious pearl of information that she was about to reveal. She looked away, focusing on some imaginary spot on the floor. "The Wishing Tree was our special place...." she began.

The story was a complete revelation to Breanna's mother. The child told her about the place of refuge that she and her older sister, Heather, had run to at the end of every day. To anyone else, it was nothing more than the useless, hollowed-out stump of an ancient juniper tree—a cavernous woody monument to what had once been. But the Lord has called all things to be part of the cycle of nature, and even in death this tree gave life—refuge—to two frightened and battered little girls.

Heather and Breanna had found an opening in this wizened massive stump that beckoned them to crawl inside to safety. There, within the hidden security of those strong wooden arms, they found escape from their fears. Inside this secret place they found what their daily life had all but destroyed—hope. Having recently escaped their violent and abusive father, they had left everything behind. All that was once familiar lay far in the distance. Now they had only each other.

But the ancient sentinel of the forest did more. It was not only a fortress from fear, but also their hideaway where the sisters could become, once again, ordinary little girls—giggling, playing, and sharing whispered secrets. There, inside that sanctuary, hope that had for so long been nearly crushed out was reignited.

Of all the dreams awakening in their young hearts, one shone brighter than the others—the desire to ride a horse. Anyone who has had the experience can understand that longing—to smell a horse's earthy fragrance, to warm your hands under a thick mane, to feel one of God's most powerful creatures beneath you, yielding to your commands with willing devotion...the sense of freedom.

This dream became their wish, their brightest star. It was for the hope of this gift that daily they would crawl into the gray snag, hold hands, and pray that somehow their wish would come true. It was this faith—the untarnished, innocent faith of two young girls—that transformed a lifeless old stump into a figurative "tree of life." If a stump could smile, I'm sure it did the first time it became known as the Wishing Tree.

Listening to the woman's barely audible voice on the phone was like hearing the weak and shallow breathing of someone near death. Exhaustion and titanic sorrow were evident in every labored sentence—she spoke with the unmistakable indicators of a severely abused and battered woman. Her name, she said, was Diane. We talked for nearly an hour as, word by word, her horrific story unfolded between us. Like a tightly gripped wad of paper, each newly revealed detail slowly and painstakingly began to reveal a crumpled self-portrait of her life of terror. Her voice was empty, weak, and timid, as if at any moment, at a poorly chosen word, a fist might crash through the telephone and slam into her jaw.

With my forehead cupped in the palm of my hand, I slumped over my desk, struggling to comprehend the violence she described. Her husband's assaults were so ferocious that she had been hospitalized fifteen times. Once, in a drunken fury, he had smashed one of her arms and her collarbone, then seized her and threw her out of a second-story window. By the grace of God, with angels rushing in, she managed to catch a railing with her unbroken arm and hold on until help arrived.

During her husband's brief imprisonment for that beating, Diane packed up her two girls and fled for her life. She drove as though chased by demons, frantically trying to put as many miles as possible between them and the man who had once vowed to love, honor, and cherish her.

Her car—equally battered and exhausted—broke down in three different states. Some incredibly generous truckers recognized her plight and, without prompting, became her guardians. Taking time away from their own hectic schedules, they made sure that she would not be stranded. Aware of her fear, they became a rolling team of strong comfort, protecting her throughout her flight. They radioed ahead and created a protective network on wheels of drivers who would safely guide the "Little Lady and her

Angels." Mile after mile, across this great country, the truckers used their rigs to pull her failing car in their own draft. Despite their differing routes, the truckers never left their post of protection until they had found another that they trusted to hand off their mantle of guardianship. Together, each doing what they could, they guided her to rest and safety.

Nearly collapsing with fatigue, Diane was at last forced to stop. They found a rundown shelter to stay in for what was left of that hellish night. Even then, the bone-weary woman felt the weight of evil eyes fixed on her as she guided her heavy-eyed daughters past the crowded rows of filthy bunk beds. But one of the men, sensing the undercurrent of danger, followed the desperate trio to their bedroom at the far end of the shelter. He had overheard her conversation at the front desk about her flight from a life of abuse.

"As a boy, I watched my mother being battered," the stranger volunteered. "No woman deserves that," he continued as his eyes dropped to the ground. "I know this is a really bad neighborhood. I want you to rest; I want you to be safe. Would you mind if I stood watch over your door tonight?" he asked with the heart of a little boy who could not do the same for his own mother. With that request, he boldly stood outside their dorm—all night long. Throughout the dark hours, the cringing family could hear him driving away evil souls who lingered at the threshold of their room, this guardian angel with the heart of a lion—a son who had grown into a man any mother would be proud of. He kept watch all night so that a haggard woman and her frightened children could finally rest.

Moving on again at first light with the continuing help of the truckers' impromptu safety network, Diane drove until they almost ran out of country—almost as far as one can go west from Louisiana. With two thousand miles behind them, she finally felt safe enough to stop in Bend, Oregon.

Once there, Diane read about Crystal Peaks Youth Ranch in a local newspaper. She confided that Heather and Breanna had pleaded with her for over a week to make this call. Her voice rose slightly as she spoke about her daughters and their long-held wish to ride. After some stammering hesitation, she added that it was Breanna's birthday the following week. Too long beaten down to have much hope for anything, she simply asked, "Would it be okay if we came?"

Immediately she backpedaled, fearing she might have presumed too much. "They don't need to ride or any-thing. Maybe," she pleaded, "they could just come out and look at the horses."

My heart ached for them. "Of course you must come," I told her, and we made the necessary arrange-ments then and there. After I hung up the phone, I sighed deeply and prayed, *Sweet Jesus, please help this little family.*

On the appointed day, I watched with quiet anticipa-tion as the two girls and their mother shyly slipped out of their car. They huddled together as they approached me, moving as though they were a single living entity. *So this,* I thought, *is the woman who has survived so much.* My first impulse was to scoop her up—to scoop them all up—in my arms, to hug them tightly as I kissed their hollow cheeks. I wanted to assure them that in this place they would always be safe; that here, both love and hope would flourish again.

But an ugly thought stopped me. They had never

known a loving touch. My first impulse to reach for them might be misconstrued—seen as a threat rather than a comfort. So I held back, greeting them with warm words, welcoming them to our little ranch. I promised them that on this day, wonderful things were going to happen.

At first the girls were hesitant to address me. I looked down into their huge brown eyes, and finally, Breanna returned my gaze. With the innocence of an angel and the hint of a smile, she said, "I am eight today."

It was a perfect opening. "Wow!" I said. "I'm honored that you would come to my ranch on such a special day. Have you ever ridden a horse before?"

Breanna shook her head gravely.

Heather, who was standing almost completely behind her mother, somberly nodded yes. But she dared not raise her eyes to look at me.

I asked gently, "You have ridden before?"

Diane turned quickly to look at Heather. In a slightly embarrassed voice she said, "Honey, please tell the truth. You've never ridden a horse in your life."

Finally, after a slight nudging from her mother's elbow, Heather lifted her head and met my eyes. With a great summoning of courage she softly said, "I ride horses every night—" her eyes quickly dropped to the ground again before she finished—"in my dreams."

Precious lamb, I thought. My eyes began to fill with tears. "Heather, did you know that sometimes dreams come true?" I said in a soft voice. "I have many horses that would love the chance to grant you your dream. Come on, let's go and meet them," I said, extending my hand toward hers. As if visually asking permission, she looked up at her mother and then back at me. Slowly, her gaze fell again to my outstretched hand. She studied it for a long moment, and then with slow deliberation, she silently put her hand in mine.

After riding two of our most gentle horses, a flicker, a glimmer, a tiny glow of hope began to emerge. And with hope, a new freedom—to play and to laugh like ordinary kids. We started out giving baths to the horses, but then, an honest "Oops, I didn't mean to squirt you" quickly erupted into a full-blown water fight with all of us tumbling around on the grass, squealing and splashing in the spray.

The rest of the day flowed by like a river of dreams, rich and lazy under a golden August sky. Past each turn and bend the girls' impish grins grew wider, melting into self-conscious giggles. Fear, which had shadowed their entire lives like a stealthy predator, could not rule them in this place. That ruthless fear was given a sound spanking and sent limping away.

Much too soon, it seemed, Diane said it was time for them to go. But first I steered them with feigned curiosity toward a white bundle I had earlier placed on one of our picnic tables. The girls undid the twisted tablecloth wrapping, and then stood back in shy surprise. Inside were all the necessary symbols of this special day—a birthday cake, cups, plates, forks...and a huge bag of carrots!

After the cake had been shared and devoured, Breanna set out at a skip with the carrots to celebrate the day of her birth with all her newfound four-legged friends. The shadows grew longer in the warm early evening, and at last it really was time for the little family to say good-bye.

I wondered if it had been enough. Had I really done my best for a family that needed so much? They had cowered for so many years under a reign of terror—could one single day really make a difference? Lost in thought, I followed their car with my eyes as it started back down the drive and through the ranch gate.

With the innocent simplicity of any eight-year-old, our birthday girl twisted in her seat to look back at me. To my great joy I saw her tiny fingers raised high, waving back at me through the car window. Caught off guard, I waved lightly in return and smiled. *Thank You, Lord. It was a good start.*

The Wishing Tree is gone—destroyed in the fire. But the hope it nurtured within its protective walls remains and continues to grow. Hope cannot be destroyed. It calls us to rise up; it whispers our name. It draws us to believe that, sometimes, wishes *do* come true.

Diane told me later that our first day together was a turning point in their lives. It was a day when hope took root and began to grow—when the fear that had held them in bondage for so long received a mortal blow. Since then, their friendship has grown deep roots in my heart. I love the sparkling silliness of the two girls whom I have come to adore as my own. They are like bricks set in the foundation of what Crystal Peaks is becoming.

I thought that first day in August was my gift to them. But in reality, by the grace of God, they have become His gift to me.

To reassure the reader, the telling of this story will not jeopardize the safety of Diane and her daughters. Diane's former husband recently died in a traffic accident.

Vitamin M

Although her name is Hailee Brite, I always think of her as Bright Hailee. Her little horseshoe-shaped grin radiates all the good cheer any heart could hope for. If sunshine could skip, it would look like Hailee. Her dark blond hair bounces behind her in golden shafts as she scans the ranch for her favorite horse. After reaching up to hug me hard, she dances off in her trademark cow-patch pants and old farmer's hat.

But before she leaves me, Hailee carries out her sweet and timeless ritual, as reliable and heartwarming as the rising sun. She bows deeply, tipping off her well-worn hat in a cascade of giggles, and presents me with the gift she has hidden inside.

Now, Hailee knows how much I enjoy cards and flowers and drawings. But she ignores all that and goes straight for what I *really* need. With all the mock drama of a court jester, she invariably produces from her hat a one-pound bag of vitamin "M."

With hearing set more finely than a tuning fork, my perceptive staff detect the delicate crinkle of plastic and converge on us at that exact moment, with all the subtlety of a tidal wave. The feeding frenzy begins—and is over in the speed of a sneeze. I'm left standing with nothing but an empty plastic bag in my hands.

Over the dispersing crowd, I smile at Hailee. She shrugs her little shoulders in a "better luck next time" gesture. I wink back at her and glance down at my mangled bag. And each time it happens I console myself by thinking, "What kind of a leader would I be...if I didn't share my M&M's?"

Chosen One

❦

ONE LOOK AT Maci would make anyone swallow hard. It was the first time that I had seen my little nine-year-old elfin since her traumatic accident. One hundred and twenty-eight stitches were needed to close what could have been fatal wounds to her face and head. Her tiny skull had been fractured with such crushing force that her parietal plate was actually displaced backward.

Now, two weeks later on this snowy January day, Maci stood in my kitchen, her bright blue eyes seemingly unaware of the savage wounds that surrounded them. She looked up at me and smiled as her tiny hands lifted up what had become a present beyond value—her riding helmet.

My whole body shivered as she carefully but triumphantly placed her completely destroyed helmet into my trembling hands. It had saved her life, this helmet. It had done its job, dispersing the impact of her fall, and now this child stood before me, alive, to give me this most precious gift. In my mind I prayed, *Thank you, Jesus, for enforcing within my heart to always protect my lambs, young and old, with riding helmets.*

Two weeks earlier, Maci and her mother had made an appointment twenty-five miles away to see a horse they were considering buying. I was out of town and the rest of our ranch leadership was unavailable, so the mother and daughter team had set out alone to test ride the horse.

Once the horse was groomed and tacked up, Maci amazed all the adults present by gently refusing to mount—because she didn't have a riding helmet. "At 'my' ranch," she said, "we are taught that the saddle goes on the horse and the helmet goes on the child. We have learned to never, ever put our foot in the stirrup without using our heads to protect our heads. I'm sorry, but I know I shouldn't ride this horse without wearing a helmet."

Maci's mother told me later how proud she was of her daughter's shy respect as she insisted on what she had been taught at Crystal Peaks. The horse's owner was able to produce a riding helmet from her garage and so, after some minor adjustments, the helmet was set firmly in place and Maci was helped into the saddle.

For nearly an hour, horse and child rode together with the perfect rhythm of a well-written poem. All too soon, though, it was time to go. Maci's mother called to her, "You look so beautiful together, honey. Why don't you canter toward us one more time?"

On their last pass the chestnut gelding was moving with fluid grace when unexpectedly he flew into a blind panic and galloped out of control. The young mother and owner waved their arms frantically, trying to make a human barricade as he thundered toward them. Using all of her strength and competence, Maci was still unable to stop the terrified horse. Neither could the adults. They were forced to dive out of the way to avoid being trampled under his flailing hooves.

The gelding careened past them at horrifying speed.

The mother and owner quickly regained their feet, only to watch helplessly as Maci and the horse disappeared from view.

Maci knew that a major crossroad with heavy traffic was fast approaching. The bloody images from the recently seen film *The Horse Whisperer* filled her mind. She knew what she must do. With the resolve of a soldier, the nine-year-old child purposefully dropped her stirrups in preparation for an emergency dismount.

No one really knows what happened next. Maci remembered a car coming out of nowhere and the horse launching himself violently to one side. Maci hit the pavement headfirst, became tangled in the horse's legs, and somehow ended up off the paved road in a ditch.

Maci's mother ran with an adrenaline-induced panic in the direction her daughter had vanished. Her recollections of those moments still flood her eyes with tears. "I looked up to see my daughter running toward me. Her scalp was hanging down in huge flaps, with blood completely covering her face and chest. As she ran, chunks of the helmet fell away. I thought it was pieces of her skull. Kim, I thought that she would run into my arms...and die."

Now, two weeks later, tears blurred my own vision as I looked down at the gift I now held. The mangled helmet was shattered beyond recognition. The Styrofoam meant to protect the front of the head was completely broken away. I could easily see the impact of where Maci's small head had recoiled and smashed out the back of the helmet. Some of the pieces were deeply embedded with rocks and cinders and smeared with blood. Trying to visualize the sheer force it would take to create this kind of damage, while cradling a child's head, made me want to vomit. I thanked the Lord again for the precious gift of the child who stood before me.

Sadly, though, I understood that physical trauma was not all that Maci had suffered. She had not only fractured her face and skull; her confidence and courage were severely damaged as well. In place of the barrel-racing fiend that I once knew, my little elfin was now afraid even to touch a rope that was connected to a horse.

Standing in my kitchen, I gently placed the shattered remains of her helmet aside and looked down past her jagged healing wounds to see her smile. "I have someone I would like you to meet," I said.

A week earlier we'd had a call from the distraught owners of two draft horses that had been shipped to a "very respected trainer" to be started under saddle. Five months later, on a cold January day, the horses—one six years old, the other two—had finally been returned to their new owners.

Joyful anticipation quickly vanished. The owners watched in disbelief as their once gentle giants backed out of the trailer into the newly fallen snow. What stood quaking before them now were two giant, young horses that had been beaten so badly that they could scarcely be touched.

And so the call came to us. "If you can fix them, you can have them."

"How could this happen?" I muttered under my breath as I went to look at the horses for the first time. I quietly entered their round pen and carefully approached Boonie, the older and larger of the two. I could see panic rising in his eyes as I gently stretched out the back of my hand. "Hey, big boy," I softly said. He shut his eyes and flung his head away from me, and his face twisted in a hard grimace as a visible shudder rolled over his body. Slowly I touched his shoulder with only the tip of my middle finger and witnessed a shock of pure terror. This giant of a horse collapsed in the hind end and literally sat down. In the face of perceived death, this was his docile response. His immense body shook as if it were in the grasp of a violent earthquake. His head jerked farther away from me, his eyes blinking rapidly before again closing tightly. It was painfully clear that he was expecting a rain of blows to his face. He thought I was going to kill him.

We moved the traumatized horses to our ranch the next day.

After a week of work, I was able to stand before my new giants and raise my hand over my head and gently return it to their heads, necks, and bodies without a significant reaction. Although still extremely wary, they were trying to trust again.

I took Maci's tiny hand in mine and shared with her the background of my new giants as we made our way down the snowy hill to our quarantine paddock for newly arrived horses.

The big geldings quietly turned to face us. They stood side by side, like pillars, watching and measuring our every movement. While I closed the gate, Maci took a few steps away from my side toward the gigantic horses. I stood fast. Casually she took another step. I watched as for the first time Boonie, who was the more damaged of the two horses, did not back up. Rather than retreating to a safe distance, he instead arched his massive neck to get a better look at my little friend. She was the first person, other than myself, that he had not moved away from. It was a huge breakthrough!

Other children had now arrived and were anxious to see our newest members of the herd. I put the giant boys out into the arena so that all could marvel at how the ground rumbled when they galloped by. They were completely magnificent! Bucking, biting, and playing, they cantered lap after jubilant lap until, exhausted, they folded their legs under them and toppled into the freshly turned sand for a lavish roll. Then lurching to their feet again, the behemoths shook mightily, throwing off clouds of sand from their steaming bodies. Both breathed heavy, contented sighs. Now they were ready to be returned to their paddock.

The children began jumping all around me in anticipation of helping put the big boys away. One child reached up and took my hand. I looked down to see Maci's scared little face peering up into mine. "Can I help?" she asked, summoning up more courage than I might ever know.

"Sure!" I said, my glib answer belying how important this moment was.

What a sight we must have been. My left hand held the end of the lead rope, my right hand firmly held Maci's left hand, and out of her right hand strung what seemed like half a mile of rope that finally led our quiet giant back to his corral.

I opened the gate and, to my surprise, Maci guided him in without me! Without looking back, she led him to the center of the corral and began reaching up to unfasten his halter. A caution rose in my throat but couldn't find enough breath to escape. My heart stopped. This violently abused horse seemed to trust her.

He was too big; she was too small. In silence she tried over and over to reach the buckle on the halter. I watched as slowly, with the gentle magnificence of a setting sun, Boonie bent his crested neck toward the earth, lowering his massive head into her tiny arms.

Unaware of the significance of what had just transpired, Maci pulled off his halter and began marching toward me, obviously proud that she had done it by herself. Quietly, the gentle giant rotated around and began to follow the little waif! A wave of words jammed up in my throat. It took a moment before my tangled tongue broke loose. "Maci, stop!" I blurted. "Boonie is following you!"

She froze as his enormous head emerged beside hers. With the gentleness of a butterfly, his huge nostrils began sniffing her face and forehead. Tenderly he explored her wounds—every stitch and scrape. He knew. Of all the children who had been in this corral, this was the only one he didn't shrink away from. This was the child he chose to trust. He seemed to understand that this child had suffered in the same ways that he had.

Without moving, her eyes rolled straight upward to look at him. She stood stiff as a wooden soldier. I could see she was afraid. His massive head was as big as her whole body. Then, seemingly satisfied, he allowed his lips to rest gently on her shoulder. Overwhelmed, I stood in silence with my hand over my mouth. Finally, my throat relaxed enough for me to speak.

"It's okay," I said. "He's loving you. You are the first person that he has chosen to trust. Out of everyone who has come to visit him, you're the one he has chosen. He must think that you're very special."

"Really?!" Her eyes widened.

"You're the chosen one," I said, my voice breaking.

In a single quiet motion, Maci turned around and slid her arms up under Boonie's double-sided mane. It was a childlike effort to hug his towering neck. In response, he bowed his head around her in an equine embrace. All that remained visible of her were her slender legs, tucked between his. My eyes dropped to see his enormous, plated feet positioned like guardians around her small, worn boots—a giant, broken horse protecting a tiny, broken child.

Even though the late afternoon light of winter had begun to fade, the child and horse shimmered like the first brilliant rays of a sunrise after a long, long storm. Somehow amid their own raging tempests, they had found each other. The impact of their embrace chiseled a permanent imprint on my heart. Tears slid down my face and silently disappeared into my fleece collar.

Maci, after contorting into a near backbend, moved her head around Boonie's neck to look at me. Her elfin face was partially concealed by the deep winter coat of his neck. She was still hugging him tightly when she asked, thoughtfully, "Do you think that I could be the one to help him get better?" I managed a nod and a smile. She contemplated that for a while before asking with the sheepishness of a nine-year-old, "When I come to the ranch, do you think that I could pretend he is my own horse?"

"I think," I said softly, "that he has already chosen you to be his special girl. I think he would like nothing better than to believe that he is your chosen boy."

Through the ebbing violet light, two broken hearts combined to form a healing flame. They seemed to warm each other from the inside out. They fit together like the mirrored halves of a bridge with their paralleled fear, pain, and hope—a horse nearly destroyed by a human, a little human nearly destroyed by a horse. No one could have understood them better than they understood each other. Each one became to the other, the chosen one.

Unchained

⚮

$\mathcal{L}$OST IN THEIR beauty, I gazed upon jagged white peaks holding up a lapis-colored sky. The Cascade mountains always made me feel stronger for simply having looked at them. Drawing a deep breath, the sweet sage fragrance of the high desert filled my senses.

My attention was jolted into the coming day by sounds of the school bus turning the corner into our long driveway and grinding its way up the hill toward the ranch. The bus exhaled a seeming sigh of relief as the driver pulled on the emergency brake and the children bounded happily off the bus. I watched their faces intently, looking for the telltale signs of a needy spirit. Excited chatter rose all around as the kids began to take in the ranch. Before welcoming the group, I quickly scanned the bus to make sure it was empty. Surprisingly, it wasn't.

Two boys were hanging in the very back, still seated, lazily pushing each other in a you-go-first manner. "Oh, *that's* Chad and Mason," a young informant said with rolling eyes.

Slowly they sauntered down the bus steps, taking their time, perfectly aware that I was waiting just for them. When they finally emerged, I was saddened by what I saw. Chad waited for Mason to step down and shoulder beside him. *For courage?* I wondered. Side by side, their posture screamed defiance as they crossed their arms over their small chests in a unified display of power.

Slouching as if there weren't a bone in their bodies, they sized me up with a meant-to-be-heard snicker. Both were dressed head to toe in baggy, black clothes. Dog chains hung from their necks and wrists. Chad had colored his fingernails with what looked like black permanent marker. Mason's hair showed the evidence of a self-inflicted haircut and black dye job—various lengths and shades of brown into black hung straight down his face, purposefully covering his eyes like symbolic bars between him and the world.

All the young teenagers were participants in an incentive program, run by a special group committed to helping kids who are failing in school—and life. These were kids who, without intervention, would not make it. This was the group that life would not wait long enough to understand. Without help they would be left behind.

For the most part they were a happy bunch, greeting me with high fives and silly handshakes as they spread out across the ranch's common area—all except Chad and Mason. They jutted out their sharp chins at me in a silent voice that shouted, "You can't control me!" The effect was diminished by the newly sprouted peach fuzz on their smooth young skin, but the message to the world was clear. "I don't need you or anyone else! Get out of my way!"

But I saw something different. My heart sank as I looked at the two hopelessly insecure boys. They were so afraid of being rejected again that they pushed everyone away first. If they could reject everyone, no one could reject them...ever again. The costumes, the postures, their attitudes all screamed it. Like a vicious dog that secretly wags its tail, they snarled, "Stay AWAY! Leave me ALONE!" But between the lines a good listener might hear their nearly inaudible whimpers, "Please, please, I don't want to be hurt anymore."

Together the boys mocked me with disparaging looks and impatient sighs. Mason relaxed his arms only to shove his hands defiantly into his baggy pockets, as if to say, "You can't make me!" Then, for the first time, he leveled his eyes on mine and taunted, "Horses are so GAY!"

It was a direct challenge of my authority. He might as well have pushed my chest and said, "What're ya gonna do about that, lady?!" *He's checking his boundaries,* I thought. *He wants me to push back. He's testing his level of power against mine to find out who the boss will be.*

Lord, I need your help now! I prayed. Wisdom is something I rarely possess. I'm sure that by now, the good Lord is used to my SOS prayers. This emergency flare went straight to heaven.

Two weeks earlier a new mare had been brought to the ranch. At twenty-three years old, she had still been in a so-called breeding program, but her low body weight, and the even lower standard of care she'd received, made carrying a foal to term impossible.

In the darkness of a cold, quiet morning her baby was lost. No one knew and no one cared. She was left to grieve alone for her stillborn infant, with nothing to comfort her but a blanket of stars overhead. The grief of her loss was overwhelming, but made incomprehensibly worse by the fact that she was left to step over her tiny lifeless foal's body for nearly two months before the stench of it finally drove someone to drag it away.

Now she was safe—but she was not well.

I looked directly back into my young challengers' eyes. "I need your help," I said simply. And I began to share with them about Elora, our devastated mare. At first the boys seemed unimpressed. But suddenly the similarities between the horse and the boys came into sharp focus. I decided to follow the list and tell the boys about...themselves.

"She was left behind by the people who were supposed to love and care for her," I said, speaking slowly and deliberately. "Her sense of trust has been destroyed, and she is struggling to overcome all the hurt that she has known. She is so broken up inside that she even keeps herself away from the other horses." I paused, observing my tough, heavy-metal boys. "She believes she is completely alone in this world. What she doesn't understand is that the prison door is open. She doesn't realize that there are many who are willing to love her back to life. All she needs is someone to help her find the way out."

All of the chained, icy black attitude began to melt into a pool somewhere below their feet. The momentary inward glimpse revealed the broken hearts of two little boys. The once-jutting lower jaws were now hanging in front of small sunken chests. They turned slightly away from each other, hiding their downcast eyes—eyes that I could see were beginning to shine with tears.

"She doesn't need a lot—just to feel loved again. Can you help me do that?" I asked. Still looking away, they both nodded.

The instructions were simple—part of our basic rehabilitation plan for every horse we rescue. Together we prepared a special pan of feed. All I asked Chad and

Mason to do was talk to her and stroke her as she ate. When I led her out from behind the barn, they were already waiting, seated on top of the picnic table. They looked so displaced, sitting in the pool of black that they had created. Their baggy clothing looked less imposing than it had at first—more like a hiding place, a camouflaged shelter to flinch behind. Their bulky chains clanked together in sharp contrast with the sound of the wind softly blowing through pine branches over their heads. Their combined heavy darkness was no match for the grassy lawn below, the endless rolling sky above, and the brilliant, laughing flowers around them.

When they first saw her, their eyes grew large and soft. Elora was a small horse, made even smaller by her diminished spirit. She moved with her head and eyes in a lowered, downcast position. She was the very picture of sorrow. Her walk was made difficult by a limp from her right front leg. From a previous unknown injury, her right knee was completely blown and permanently swollen to nearly twice its normal size. She quietly began eating from their laps, the boys neither moved nor spoke. I silently coiled Elora's lead rope and laid it on the table beside them. Smiling softly, I backed away.

Forty-five minutes later, the ranch was alive with leaders, children, and horses. Dust rose like a great halo over the arena. Although days like these are a tremendous amount of work, the joy far outweighs the job.

I started to make my way back to the boys. Although Chad had gone on to other activities, through the rising dust I could see the once black-haired Mason alone with the mare. I stopped. He was gently holding each of her rounded cheeks as she rested her chin on his thighs. His lips were moving and his face was very close to hers. I watched him, over and over, repeat this loving cycle—tenderly leaning his forehead against Elora's and whispering, then pulling back and kissing her face.

The mare's eyes were nearly closed. From where I stood, I watched as two hearts made their way toward the light of newfound hope. In my own heart I could hear chains falling to the ground. The prisoners were going free. For a long while I silently watched before wiping my eyes and approaching them.

Mason rolled his head to look at me, his eyes warm and tender. His cheek was resting between Elora's closed eyes. He smiled. My heart melted. I put my hand over my mouth and was thankful for sunglasses. I'm sure he knew I was crying.

I climbed up onto the table and sat next to them and put my hand on Mason's back. When I was able, I quietly said, "Look what you've done."

He looked up at me. The heavy metal juvenile was gone. In his place sat a young boy with unruly hair, dressed in black, loving a destitute horse. "You showed her it's okay to trust again. You showed her how to open the door." I smiled at him. "Mason, you did it."

hope
rising
in the
midst
of fire

Fear Knot

❦

I AM NO carpenter, but in the last handful of years I have hammered down thousands of nails. My tool belt swagger matches that of the best journeymen. I have abused to destruction more DeWalt drills than I wish to confess, and I am certain that I have spent more time eyeballing lengths of wood than buying food at the market. I've even grown to enjoy the fragrant allure of lumberyards and learned from those more experienced than I, the art of long-eyeing each board.

Every piece of wood must be lifted to allow a visual and tactile check of dryness, balance, and straightness. Then it is eyed down its length to see if it is true—not warped or bowed in any way. But this comes only after the board has passed a visual knot test. Experienced carpenters know that knots weaken the wood around them. Knots, typically, are viewed as flaws. And human nature usually dictates that the more flaws something has, the more it is to be avoided.

At the ranch we are constantly in need of true one-by-twelve-inch barn boards—the longer the better—for constructing and repairing the many outbuildings. One hot September day I decided to go in search of lumber to finish the upper wind shelters.

Clean and straight one-by-twelves can be hard to

find—most lumberyards do not have enough demand to keep them in stock. Sorting through stacks of assorted heavy boards has taught me what a blessing it is to find what I need on top. But this day it was a frustrating search. At first I thought, shifting a massive sixteen footer, *Ah well, the Lord loves variety. What an uninteresting world it would be if everything were perfect.* But this whole stack was a bust. Every board was full of knots.

"Defective! Defective! Defective!" I muttered, rubbing grimy hands on my jeans. There was nothing. Not one keeper in the entire lot. It was a little discouraging, knowing how badly I needed the lumber and how high the prices were. I picked out the best knotty boards I could find, paid, and headed back to the ranch.

We had rescued the two-year-old bay colt and his chestnut half-brother in July. Both were stunted in growth and grossly underweight. The bay's skeletal body also had been stricken with chronic diarrhea, a condition that often signifies a lethal slide toward death. All his legs tended to collapse toward his center in a pitiful attempt to support his frail body.

But the bay didn't die. In eight weeks he gained nearly a hundred pounds. We called him Lazarus because his initial condition had been so bad that he appeared, almost literally, to have been raised from the dead.

At first, Lazarus was uncertain of human touch—common behavior, we have come to recognize, for a starving horse who turns all his focus inward. But as his strength increased, so did the expression of his mischievous personality. He grew rapidly into a silly ranch clown.

Scratching Lazarus is always a trigger for laughter because he does something I've never seen before. Most horses express pleasure by pushing their upper lip forward in a kind of equine smile. Lazarus does just the opposite, pulling his lip backward until it flattens against his teeth. If someone really tickles him, he wiggles his flattened lip from side to side like a rabbit.

His sweet baby face draws kids like a magnet, so I like to include him when I give tours of the ranch. Once when I was showing several girls around, I told them about Lazarus on the way to visit him. The staff and I have come to realize that children bond with horses more quickly when they know the animal's background and have had a proper introduction.

Lazarus was being true to his goofy form. After encouraging us to scratch him thoroughly, he decided to finish the job himself by rolling around inside his wind shelter. Every time he rolled over he tried to rub his face on the wall. When that didn't satisfy him, he stretched his legs out straight, which only pushed him farther from the wall. Then—I don't know if he was entertaining himself or us—he used the wall as a springboard to flip himself back over again.

We watched Laz repeat this silliness several times before moving on. Our little group was heading toward the corral gate when we heard his banging and thumping against the wall grow louder. Afraid that he might have gotten stuck in a position from which he couldn't stand up again, I backtracked and peeked around the wall of the shelter. Laz was still lying down, but he could easily get up if he wanted to. He turned to look at me, his head lolling back. His playful brown eyes seemed to twinkle with a convincing look that said, "I didn't do anything wrong." I laughed and shook my head at him.

I jogged back down the path toward my group of girls when another loud crash snapped my head around. The colt's front hoof had hit the bottom of a one-by-twelve so hard that it tore loose the screws holding it in place. Not amused, I wheeled around, intending to roll him up and shift him to something less expensive to destroy. Before I could take another step, his entire front leg shot through the new opening.

Instantly I knew the scenario, and adrenaline jolted me like an electric shock. *Please, Jesus, help!* flashed through my mind. The situation had exploded from annoying to life threatening. Horses are animals of flight—their instinct is always to run from danger first, to reason later. Lazarus would panic the moment he knew his leg was trapped. He would pull with as much force as it took to free himself, even if it meant breaking his leg or literally pulling off his hoof, which is not as rare as it sounds. Such an injury cannot be fixed and nearly always means certain death.

My body felt caught in a slow-motion dream. I was running, but I couldn't move fast enough. I had to get to Laz before he started to pull his leg back through the narrow gap between the loose board and the bottom four-by-four that had once anchored it.

His leg began to disappear into the gap—until the heavy board closed firmly above his hoof. I saw his leg pull back—a trial movement that confirmed he was stuck. In a single heartbeat his panic rose into a violent series of bone crushing jerks.

Lord! my heart screamed. *Help us! He's going to pull his foot off!* All I could hear was my own pulse hammering against my eardrums. I lunged forward as though through quicksand toward the trapped colt. His fear crescendoed into an explosion of frenzied panic. Pain was searing through his leg with a grip that he could not escape. In rising terror, he launched a final burst of sheer force. In one last Herculean jerk—it was over. Shards of splintered wood flew toward my face as the heavy board shattered.

I nearly fell into the wind shelter. "Laz!" I cried, reaching out to calm him. Almost too afraid to look, my eyes followed the length of his leg down to his hoof. Amazed but grateful, I saw that his hoof was still attached.

Within minutes, Shawn, one of our most supportive and dear veterinary friends, arrived to examine Lazarus. To my great relief, he said that no vital or permanent damage had been done. The colt had a gash that went right down to the bone, but Shawn assured me it looked worse than it was. He stitched it neatly while I cradled Laz's baby face against my chest and stroked his forehead. I shuddered to think what would have happened if the board hadn't broken when it did.

Watching Shawn's steadfast expertise as he sutured the wound, listening to him patiently explain his every move to a fascinated little boy who was watching, I felt the adrenaline high drain from my body. Relief washed over me. The knowledge that Lazarus was all right flowed out of me like a deeply held breath.

At last, Shawn wrapped the sutured cut, and I led Lazarus back to his paddock. *Lord, he's just a baby,* I thought, looking down at his tiny hooves. My brain shut down abruptly. That board was fully one inch thick and twelve inches wide. How could a stunted little horse, only recently rescued from starvation, shatter such a monstrous plank?

After settling Lazarus into his paddock, I went back to investigate the accident scene.

I didn't have to look far for the answer. Picking up the shattered end of the board, I felt a deep and sudden sense of the miraculous. In the entire wall of the wind shelter, this was one of the few boards that was imperfect. One of the few boards that had a huge knot in it. Without that blessed imperfection, my little colt would probably have died.

I thought back to that day at the lumberyard and my frustration with all the flawed boards. In my worldly way, I had sought perfection, thinking it would best serve my purposes. Society teaches us that anything less than perfect is unsuitable, undesirable, unusable, and unattractive— that it should be avoided whenever possible. But pure reality teaches us that the Lord loves and uses the flawed, unattractive, and broken—the apparently useless things of this world—to accomplish His greatest works.

As many as all the nails I have hammered are the times I have scolded myself for my shortcomings. It is easy to become focused on our "defective" areas and completely miss all that they teach us. Our flaws, our imperfections motivate us to become pliable, moldable, and teachable. And like knots in wood, they give us our uniqueness and character. They help to bend or even break us to the point where we are able to recognize the needs of others and to help them.

Now when I marvel at the majesty of the trees in my native forest, I see things differently. And if I really listen, I can hear the Maker laugh and say, "See, My child, I made the knots, too!"

Little Things

THE FOUR-LEGGED staff at Crystal Peaks Youth Ranch work the hardest. They love every child with all they have, frequently building bridges into wounded lives where adults are not yet allowed. Often, the walls of destruction surrounding a child's heart are broken down beneath their trusted hooves.

Because the horses give so much for so little, we try hard to always have a "good horse" supply of carrots. It is just something we do, a small detail, a little thing.

Unfortunately, time restraints often force us to overlook the simple things of life and focus our efforts on the siren call of what *must* be done. Although necessary, we can lose sight of the blessing that so many of the little things bring us.

Such was this particular summer day—a blur of tousled heads and toothy grins. And then I realized, *We need more carrots*. It was more of a thought than a prayer. But God must have heard me....

"I'll be right back," I called over my shoulder to the staff as I made my way up the hillside to our house. While retrieving more film, I decided to check for phone messages at the same time. During the summer season, Crystal Peaks Youth Ranch receives forty or more phone calls per day. This day one message in particular got my attention. I dialed the given number. After a pleasant exchange of information, I returned back down the hill with a crude map in my hands.

"As soon as someone sees Troy drive up, would you please send him my way?" I asked. Soon after, Troy chugged up the driveway. I met him with map in hand and a simple request.

"I received a sweet phone call today. It was a total stranger asking if we could use some carrots in our program. Isn't that great?"

Not really knowing what to expect, I wanted to make sure that this simple gift was honored. I had assured the caller that we would come as quickly as we could spare the manpower and a truck. Although the gift was quite a distance away, Troy agreed to make the trip. Armed with a tall Mason jar of ice tea, he climbed back up into the cab. I secretly hoped the long drive would be a relaxing finish to his day, instead of becoming one more thing to accomplish on an already superhuman schedule.

Later in the afternoon the sun had slipped closer to the western horizon. When shadows began to lengthen toward the east, the staff and I began our evening ritual of ranch pickup and feeding the herd.

We were midway through this task when from down below, nearly a quarter of a mile away, I recognized the sound of our truck's straining engine. I continued to listen as Troy rounded the turn that led up to Crystal Peaks. The engine complained loudly as the truck struggled up the hill. Puzzled by the labored sound, I tossed out the last flakes of hay and turned around to see what all of the grumbling was about.

My jaw nearly bounced off my chest—I couldn't *believe*

it! Like a four-wheel-drive Atlas, our truck staggered beneath the nearly impossible load. The front tires were barely in contact with the ground. "Oh my gosh!" I laughed out loud as Troy could barely steer the truck into the main yard. He was laughing, too.

Stewart, our new friend who had called earlier in the day, knew a farmer who grew seed carrots. Apparently, this was only a portion of his surplus.

The staff and I formed a makeshift brigade as Troy threw down the forty-five-pound gunnysacks from above. We continued stacking the sacks in the barn until there was a mountain of carrots so large that it would have nearly filled a stall—the total added up to about 2500 pounds!

After the job was finished, we all stepped back and looked with completely dumbfounded expressions at the monument we had just created. All we could do was stand there and laugh.

I told the staff about my prior thoughts of needing more carrots, although I never voiced it to the Lord or to them because it was just a little thing.

A simple thought crashed into my mind as if being hit by a one-ton wall of carrots. How completely wonderful to have a God who knows what we need even before we know. He answers our prayers even before they are prayed. He cares about the big things...and the little things.

Run Through Fire

IT WAS OUR last training ride before the beginning of the endurance-racing season. Under the long light of the evening sun, Sarah and I cantered shoulder to shoulder up the dusty road, moving in unison to the ancient, rhythmic beat of drumming hooves.

Though only fourteen, Sarah was already my dear friend and faithful riding partner. Through a series of devastating events, her life had become deeply entwined with mine. Her tender age lagged far behind her level of maturity. To some, she was a child, a lanky waif, a shy apparition, seen but not heard. To me, she had quietly developed into one of my deepest and truest friends. She knew that I loved her beyond any mistake or misjudgment she could ever make. In the glow of that knowledge, she had grown into a quietly confident ranch-building force. In turn, she represented the embodied love of Christ for me. She understood my heart, my desire to love the downtrodden, the underdogs, the unnoticed souls who slip through the cracks of life.

Sarah had always found it difficult to share her heart, but she communicated her devotion silently, powerfully, through ceaseless action. Our common love for horses had drawn us even closer. Riding with Sarah that day, I looked across at her cantering beside me, her trademark pigtails rising and falling in time with her young horse's hooves, and thought that nothing else on earth could have satisfied my heart more at that moment.

In the low, dusty light, Sarah glanced at me and grinned. That was it! Pure joy couldn't be stifled. At a near gallop I dropped the tethered reins on my horse's neck, threw my arms into the sky, and shouted with laughter. Without hesitation, she followed suit. From somewhere behind us, angels may have sped to keep up while giggling at the sight of these two joyful silhouettes, their jubilant forms barely perceptible through the rising layer of creamy dust as they galloped toward an orange sherbet sky. The lazy dust lingered in its destined fall back to earth, while joyful whoops and laughter could be heard in the distance. Joy was being carried on an evening breeze to all creation before sleep, the embracing reminder that life is good.

It was during that poignant moment that I saw the first glimmer, the first release of emotion, from Sarah's guarded heart.

Our faithful horses began to cool out, walking shoulder to shoulder, and I vowed to Sarah that we would do the same thing in the race. No matter what we might encounter during this experience, we would face it side by side.... We would give our very best and then finish...shoulder to shoulder.

Sarah pondered my words for a long moment. Finally she looked away. Her emotions were so guarded, so deep—churning like a subterranean river through caverns of stone. All too often she retreated into a locked silence.

Her internal conflict was evident in her downcast eyes. I could tell all that she held inside, all that she wanted to express was reaching toward the surface, straining desperately to be free. It was agonizing to watch.

After long moments she finally looked back at me. I could see that her internal dam was crumbling beneath the weight of what she wanted to say. Then, like a life-giving spring seeping to the surface in a high mountain meadow, the words began to flow.

"You know what would really be great?" Her voice was barely audible as her gaze dropped to the ground. "When we cross the finish line...will you...hold my hand?" Silence. Her soft green eyes were veiled by her eyelashes as she continued to look down. She seemed to be whispering to herself as she added, "That...would be the *best.*"

Through the long shadows of the evening, I reached my hand across the gap that separated us. She reached back and laced her slender fingers through mine. Her slight Mona Lisa smile could have split rock! Actually, I'm quite certain that it did. A gust of wind, like the draft from angels' wings, swirled dust across the road before us. My heart caught the zephyr and soared through the delicious colors of the sky as we continued to ride side by side, hand in hand.

Now it was three days later, the day before the endurance race. We carefully trailered our team of five horses, five riders, and what seemed like enough equipment to outfit an army. Slowly we wove through a sea of approximately two hundred horses and all of the necessary accoutrements. To admit that it was a little intimidating would be an understatement. Not only was this the largest race that we had done so far, but also my young partner's parents were coming. For the first time they would see their daughter race.

Sarah's parents were hardworking, simple people who had sacrificed the time to pack up their old Volkswagen van and come to the race. The camp was in foothills that reached to nearly six thousand feet, and though the days were warm, once the sun dropped below the mountainous skyline the temperature would plunge without mercy until it slipped into the teens. I knew Sarah was concerned about her parents' comfort, apprehensive of how her horse would perform, and most anxious about their approval of all the work she had accomplished to get to this moment. Would they be pleased? She never expressed her worries, but they flooded her countenance nevertheless.

After hastily setting up camp, we shifted into the relaxing rhythm of grooming the four-legged half of our team. We took great pride in this process, knowing that all of our horses but one had been rescued—not purchased for their perfection, but for their need. Two of them had nearly starved to death. Another had been beaten so violently by her former owner that a vet was needed to sew up her innocent face. Now, between her eyes, a diagonal scar six inches long was a reminder of that vicious attack. The fourth one had been in such a desperate state that we'd driven through a black, howling blizzard over an unplowed mountain pass to get him to our vet. Even as Curt, our dear veterinary friend, worked on him, he quietly prepared us for his death.

Years of abuse had left two of our horses with serious disfigurements. One carried a jagged ten-inch scar across his shoulder. The other, a mare, bore the evidence of a nine-inch gash that twisted down her right front cannon bone, or shin, and ended in an egg-sized lump of proud flesh above the coronet band, just above the hoof. The two other horses survived incredible neglect. One, being denied the nutrition needed during her formative years, had slightly, but permanently, bucked knees.

This was our team.

Our deep pride in grooming these horses arose from their former lack. For their sheer will and courage alone, they deserved more than we could ever give them. Only after they had been thoroughly bathed, brushed, and combed, gleaming under the sun like fine polished metal, were they ready.

We led them into the prerace vet check area, where we moved like a tiny tributary into a vast river of horses. They were nearly all Arabians, exotic, athletic, proud, and bold—lean powerful horses that we couldn't imagine had ever known a day of hunger or the threat of abuse.

Our team was quickly noticed and targeted by the usual looks—the silent comparison of our horses with theirs, an attitude that slithers its way insidiously, like a black serpent, through the milling horses and up and down each imperfect leg, over every scarred back. Some of the other competitors gestured at us, pointing and murmuring. A few attacked us openly, loudly voicing their bitter opinion of me and my equine refugees. Some were vindictive enough to say to my face that they hated me, how only horses like theirs should be allowed to race.

It could be devastating.

Thankfully, the vast majority of the time we were greeted with great kindness and warmth, particularly by those who had lent their generous support to our equine rescue program and our limited-distance endurance team. So we reassured ourselves by concentrating on our veterinarians' opinions, remembering the highly focused training we had put in to get this far, and reminding ourselves that scars are evidence of the trials of life, a testament to victory over adversity. We were confident that within each of our horses' battered exteriors burned the heart of a lion.

Friday afternoon of any weekend endurance race is the major prerace vet check, which determines whether a horse is fit to race the following morning. It's the same at every race—the horses are called from a lineup, one at a time, by a hardworking vet who checks their vital signs, hydration factors, back, girth, tendons, and hoofs. Notes are taken on every horse as a baseline for the mid and postrace checks. The last phase is a trotout, where the vet analyzes the horse's gait. Any imbalance, no matter how slight, means the horse is not fit to continue and is immediately pulled from the race.

One after the other our horses entered the vet check area, and the members of our team quietly explained their mount's story of survival. As always, the vets listened with compassion, making careful notes of every bump and scar on the competitor's scorecards. Often they congratulated our young riders with hearty hugs of approval for working so hard to rehabilitate horses that might have otherwise died.

Four of our five horses had cleared the vet check. I stood and waited for Sarah as she and her "boy," Mighty Mojave, entered the vetting area. Sarah had fallen in love with the horse when he was a yearling, living down the road on a local ranch. She was only a little girl then, but because of him, she sought employment on the ranch as a groom. He was so small for his age that his exotic gray face seemed too diminutive to support such incredibly large dark eyes. He and Sarah's young hearts were soon inseparable.

Then the season of lack struck. His infant body could not bear the lean rations, and his weight began to plummet. Sarah watched helplessly through the fence as he slipped closer toward the gnawing jaws of starvation. As often as she dared, she slipped her young soul mate food and water and spent many frozen winter hours stroking his beautiful face, whispering comfort to his hungry heart.

Winter gave way to the resilient power of spring, and that same life-giving force took hold of Sarah's heart. Like tender shoots of grass pushing through a sidewalk, she resolved with all the strength of an eleven-year-old to do whatever it took to rescue her boy. So began for her an entire year of mucking out stalls and paddocks, bathing, grooming, riding, feeding, and the myriad of other chores on a large breeding ranch. She did it all for a year...for free. Her only payment at the end would be the little runt of a gray colt.

Sarah and Mojave grew up together in the unmatched harmony so common between a girl and a horse. Through the long summer afternoons when she hung on his back or napped by him in the pasture, he flourished in the radiant shelter of her love. She started training him alone without a buck or a hitch, riding him gently to gradually build up his fledgling strength. The once-emaciated waif was gone. In his place stood a powerful fifteen-hand silver horse. His head was still uniquely Arab; his expressive eyes were still the largest I had ever seen, but they were different. Instead of being overcast brown pools reflecting hollow uncertainty, now they reflected only her. She was his life, from beginning to end. All of his focus and affection was finely tuned to a single point. He saw only her. I was certain that for Sarah, this magnificent horse, without hesitation, would run through fire.

She saved him. Now, in her uncertain teenage years, he was saving her. When Sarah entered the vetting area, she handled her horse with casual confidence. He was an extension of her. Sarah and the vet talked easily. The local vet remembered this horse and his remarkable story. The scorecard slowly filled with A's. Now would come the routine trot out. I glanced at my watch and looked up. My jaw dropped, and I stared in disbelief.

It was nearly imperceptible, but unmistakable—a tiny rhythmic bob of Mojave's beautiful head. I watched, holding my breath, as he was rechecked and trotted out again. The minute rise and fall of his head persisted—a clear indication that something was wrong.

My stomach twisted into a sick knot. I had a strong professional background in sports physiology, and I trained our horses the way I trained athletes. Our team's training was consistent, progressive, and precise, and included speed, distance, and incline components. Consequently, our horses had little, if any, incidence of injury. Only days before, Mojave had been a virtual distance-devouring machine.

What had happened?

I could only watch with a deflated heart as Sarah's scorecard was handed back to the attending vet and Mojave was pulled from the race lineup. The vet reassured Sarah that the lameness was mild enough that the horse might possibly return to soundness within the afternoon. He encouraged her to bring Mojave back for a recheck later in the evening. Even so, Sarah rejoined the team with enormously sad eyes set within a very pale face.

I knew she was thinking of her parents, making the long journey just to watch her race. Would it be for nothing? She didn't want to disappoint them, but her silent demeanor on the way back to our camp showed that she felt she already had.

Once again, Sarah and I worked side by side. Together, we wrapped Mojave's lame leg with what little ice we had. When that had melted, we formed a bucket brigade to the central water tank of the race camp, keeping the leg cool with hand-poured water. The afternoon passed slowly as we made trip after trip, hauling the heavy sloshing tubs of water, hoping to restore a little horse...and a dream.

Sarah was in more pain than Mojave. It was devastating to see the storm of concern and anxiety building behind her silent expression. After deep consideration, I called our small team together. In a circle of combined hearts and hands, I prayed aloud a simple prayer for the healing of Sarah's horse. I asked the good Lord that His answer would come in such a way that everyone would know it was His great love that made the difference. In the midst of hugs and tears, a cool breeze swirled between us—an unseen messenger that seemed to ferry our simple prayer up through the forested hillside and into the very presence of God.

It was early evening when a Volkswagen van rattled up the dusty road toward our camp. Sarah's parents had arrived. She approached them with the body language of a girl preparing to show her parents a failing report card.

After a brief and quiet conversation with them, she returned to her post at Mojave's shoulder and continued his restorative care. She was exhausted, emotionally and physically. Her vigil continued through the cool evening into the cold night. Twice she led her gelding the half mile to the vet check area, and twice he was declared still slightly lame. When it was dark and the area was illuminated only by headlight beams, the vet finally encouraged her with, "Come back around five-thirty in the morning, and we'll look at him one more time." She nodded in silent agreement as she cradled her horse's head in her arms.

Fatigue drew all of us toward our frigid tents, but before turning in, I asked Sarah to wake me so that we could go to the early morning check together. Through heavy eyes and an even heavier heart, she promised she would. I watched her small flashlight beam retreat like a lonely star as she made her way to her tent.

The night passed all too quickly in dreamless sleep. I woke to a gray morning, my icy breath drifting up to join a thick layer of frozen condensation on the inside of the tent walls. Thin layers of ice had fallen onto my sleeping bag during the night.

Thankfully, I had stuffed most of my clothes into my sleeping bag to stay warm. The trick now was to dig them out and get them on without knocking down the layer of ice hanging precariously over my head. That accomplished, I crawled out of the tent and glanced at our portable corral.

We were one horse short. Mojave was gone. And so, I discovered, was Sarah.

Quickly I pulled on my boots and riding gear. Light was only just beginning to tint the eastern horizon. The long valley that stretched down toward the main camp and vetting area was filled with a smoky mist. The ground and every living thing that covered it were dressed in a woolly layer of heavy silver frost. Earth and sky blended almost seamlessly into a shimmering veil of gray. Pulling on my gloves, I scanned the milky valley for any movement. My feet crunched on the frozen grass as I took a few steps, straining my eyes. Finally, through the sea of gray, a form started to emerge...then two. I watched as they materialized into dark gray shapes.

They walked shoulder to shoulder with their heads down. Occasionally, without looking up, Sarah rested her right hand on Mojave's mane. Their combined body language was either of extreme relief...or despair. I continued to study them as they approached, anxious for any sign, any clue that might hint at either negative or positive news. But they revealed nothing, moving like floating phantoms up the streaming silver river of frost beneath their feet.

My body wouldn't move, my lungs wouldn't fill. I was afraid to blink. *Lord, this is so important to a young heart....* My rambling prayer ended abruptly as her head slowly came up and she saw me.

I felt like a statue, welded into this somber place. My hands were buried deep in my pockets. My frozen breath rose silently around me. Time seemed to freeze as well. I could feel my heart pounding in my ears. Sarah held my gaze across the distance between us. I struggled to make out the features of her face. A crisp breeze swirled down toward me as if carrying from heaven my answer within its wings. Then Sarah raised her arms high into the frosty air and threw her head back in a victorious gesture, like an Olympian who had just won gold. My heart leaped! I wanted to scream for joy; I wanted to fall to my knees; I wanted to cry. But most of all, I wanted to thank the Lord for answering the simple prayer of a little girl.

We ran to each other, meeting in an embrace so warm that it dashed the wintry grip of the morning. Our hearts rose high with the sun, matching the first golden lasers of light illuminating the blanket of mist. We sprinted back to camp, which was by now abuzz with excitement, and the morning whirled past with final race preparations. It hardly seemed more then a few moments before our team was saddled, mounted, and warmed up.

The horses' jubilant strides mirrored the hearts of their riders. They couldn't wait to begin, respectfully letting us know that they were nearly bursting to gallop, to fill their nostrils with wind, to stretch their God-given wings and fly through the forested mountains.

The countdown began—three, two, one, GO!

Without hesitation, our well warmed horses leaped into a powerful gallop. Incredible strength rose beneath us, gaining speed and power with each lengthened stride until gravity itself strained to hold us earthbound.

Pure horsepower in its most extreme sense expanded and contracted beneath us. With wind-whipped tears streaming back through my hair, I felt my mare's power thunder with such remarkable force that in those moments, she felt more like an iron locomotive than a beast of flesh and blood. Gravity snapped, and we soared free of earthly bonds. Racing on the wings of the wind...we flew!

The once placid trees blurred past us into a fluid emerald forest. The strong headwind created by our resounding flight spirited away our laughing voices into the recesses of the wilderness. Joy shimmered throughout the air, cascading like droplets onto the forest floor behind us. The trees bent and waved back in the midst of our draft, cheering us on with waving boughs. In our wake, I imagined our laughter turning the silver blanket of frost into pure gold.

Miles ticked by like minutes. Gradually we reined in our horses until they settled into a big, fluid trot that powered us up one mountainous ridge after another. Each seemed to rise forever toward the deepening blue sky, only to crest and roll back down in majestic, shady folds of deep green. Above the muffled cadence of our horses' hooves over the humus floor, the whispering voice of the forest could be heard. Breezes hushed in the tops of the trees seemed to call us by name. The forest opened its enfolded arms and welcomed us into its timeless evergreen embrace.

Eventually the land sloped down and away, bending toward a creek. The midrace vet check was less than half a mile down the trail. We dismounted and led the horses the remaining distance. When we walked into the vet check area, Sarah's expression changed from deep, quiet joy into something more somber. We both understood that whatever had affected Mojave before could return after his exertion.

To begin the vet checking procedure, the horse's heart rate must first return to a resting rate of sixty beats per minute. Mojave's pulse, when it was checked at the water trough, was already there. I watched over my mare's back as step by step the attending vet began to check off his list of crucial elements. The young gelding passed each one with high scores.

It was time for the trot out.

Would Mojave pass? If he was declared sound and released, Sarah would be able to finish the race—within sight of her parents. I held my breath as he began to trot—twenty yards away from the vet and then back again. The vet's back was to me; his head slowly dropped as he looked down. I could see Sarah's wide eyes searching his face for the answer, and then she looked down, too. The vet was scrawling something across her competitor's card.

A breeze stirred Ele's mane over the back of my hands. I glanced at them and suddenly realized that my hands were pressed against her neck in tight white fists. I closed my eyes and exhaled. *I trust in You, Lord*, I mouthed into the fluttering mane.

I looked up just as the vet finished writing. He held onto the scorecard for a moment, speaking to Sarah. I stared at her face intently, straining to interpret her expression. Suddenly, her beautiful lips spread into a smile. The vet returned her card and gave her a thumbs up. She looked straight at my face. Her expression etched a permanent portrait in my heart. It was a look I'll never forget.

We met in a huge embrace. "He passed!" she exhaled into my hair, as if she, too, had been holding her breath. "He *passed*."

Ele's heart rate took slightly longer to come down, so Sarah passed the vet check ahead of me. She rode out, with a grinning promise over her shoulder that they would ride slowly until we caught up.

When Ele was released, she seemed to eat the course one long-legged bite at a time. At every turn I watched for Sarah until finally she and her gray boy came into view. Our horses drew up shoulder to shoulder and began to prance with excitement. Fueled by their own fiery passion, they galloped up the mountainside like an uphill avalanche. Each breath seemed to fill them with more energy, more desire, and more power. We charged out into a clearing and were stunned by the beauty of the world far below us. In a near unison declaration of joy, Sarah and I whooped and screamed together. Our announcement echoed through the thin high air, ringing with the gifts of life.

Our horses, faithfully, side by side, climbed until there was nothing left to climb. Then, almost abruptly, a sign announced that the finish was half a mile ahead. We dismounted as before and began walking. Strategically, we allowed our horses' heart rates to drop, knowing that the race is only finished after you have crossed the finish line and your horse's heart rate has dropped to sixty beats or less.

The finish came into view, and we were both suddenly aware of how quiet it was. There were no other horses and few people in a normally crowded area. Hand in hand we crossed the finish line together.

Sarah's beaming mother was the first to greet us with open arms. Her father moved in to capture the scene on film through the eyes of a professional photographer, snapping one photo after another while mother and daughter hugged tightly.

My young partner was glowing, basking in the love of her parents and the incredible effort and sense of accomplishment that she shared with her horse. With a brilliant smile, her mother exclaimed while nearly shaking her, "Baby, you won! *You won!*" Sarah's mouth broke into a wide open smile as she hugged her mom with one arm and her horse with the other.

It was the best of days, shared with her family and friends...and her horse—her little gray runt whose starved body and heart were restored by the power of her love.

It was a reminder that every now and then if we work hard enough and dream hard enough something wonderful happens. Hope can *not* be stopped. There are times when the fiery walls of reality are not strong enough, hot enough, or high enough to stop a dream fueled by hope from crashing through. Dreams drive through flames that scar, burn, melt—and forge us into the creatures God wants us to be. Dreams driven by hope, empowered by love, change us forever.

Of the fifty-two competitors that ran the twenty-five mile race, our little team of rescued horses placed first, second, third, sixth and seventh! Sarah, on her silver gelding Mighty Mojave, won the Junior Division and the Junior Best Condition Award. She was the overall champion and set a blistering course record that has yet to be beaten.

I always believed that Mojave would run through fire for Sarah. On that day—he did.

Easy Keeper

"MOMMY, IS THAT a cow or a horse?" the little boy asked. He stood only a few feet away from the stocky chestnut gelding.

Cappy is known as an "easy keeper." Easy keeping horses are those that eat an ordinary amount of hay and immediately go down the path of "once on the lips, forever on the hips."

Even with a restricted feeding program, horses like Cappy are usually chronically obese. Whatever he eats might as well be pasted on his belly because that's where it all seems to go.

"Well, honey, what do *you* think?" the mother answered as she returned the question back to the boy. With his little eyebrows knit together in concentration, the child gazed up at the mighty chestnut girth looming above him.

The young mother prompted, "Do you think that he looks more like a cow or more like a horse?" The child's visual examination continued with intense scrutiny.

Too much time had passed. He didn't seem to like either of his choices. Perhaps he felt that it was a trick question.

Suddenly, his eyebrows bolted straight up with the apparent resolution of his conflict. Jamming his little hands over his little hips in triumph, he looked back toward his mother wearing an irrepressible grin. With wisdom he declared his final conclusion: "I think he looks more like a PIG!"

hope
rising
through
ashes

Refuge

HE WOMAN'S voice on the other end of the phone line was somber. "Her mother has died. It's only been three days..." Instantly my heart traveled back to another time, another place, to one of those memories we have, but try to forget. I vividly remembered that moment in my own life....

"Honey, your parents have died." The words seared into my nine-year-old heart. In the blur of that moment, I knew someone was trying to comfort me, but all I wanted was to get away, to run as far as I could from this hideous truth. Tearing away from the arms that held me, I burst out through the back door of the house and ran. I ran and ran through a small orchard. The short distance felt like miles until finally I fell, face down, into the powdery, dry earth. I could hear screaming, only to realize that it was my own unrecognizable voice—the cry of a child's heart that was trying to comprehend the incomprehensible.

I loved both of my parents with all of the passion of a child's heart, yet divorce was tearing them apart. My dad sought help in many professional directions, but, tragically, help was not to be found. With a decision conceived through blinding despair, he grimly ended my mother's life and then his own.

Silence. At long last there was silence. All that was left of my shattered voice whispered the simple words, "Jesus, help me." A near silent breeze moved through the leafless branches overhead.

In that moment, looking down through the lifeless trees, angels might have seen deep knee prints forming in the dusty earth next to a small, huddled form. It was there in that barren place that the Lord of all knelt to comfort a broken child. In that instant my life was saved. Not fully understanding all that had happened inside my heart, what I felt, what I knew was that I would never again be alone.

After the death of my parents, I moved in with my grandparents. It wasn't long before they had the foresight to buy a small horse for me. Between the love of the Lord and that little horse, Firefly, I found a refuge in my shattered life. Riding became my place of safety and peace. No matter how difficult things were, my troubles could never catch me when I was on Firefly.

Most days I jumped off the school bus and ran as fast as I could down the road that led to our house. I tore off my school clothes as I ran into the house and yanked on old jeans as I ran out. I couldn't get to my little mare fast enough. Tears can wait only so long. I was convinced that there was no better place to cry than on Firefly's soft neck. Certainly I couldn't have wished for a better listener. She always seemed to understand my broken heart. She never judged me. Instead, she carried me away to a place where the hurt was not swift enough to keep up.

We rode so fast that my tears were whipped dry from my face. We would wind through the brushy forest to leave behind the pain that tried to destroy my heart. By playing my imaginary game of hide and seek, my pain was soon lost far behind. Only then was my heart free to soar.

For many years my favorite place to ride was an oak forest not far from home. The trees were immense. I used to think that it would take an entire family, holding hands, to reach around each massive trunk. Their gigantic spreading branches arced across the sky, weaving into each other as if they were holding hands in a mighty celebration of life itself. Beneath their shady expanse all kinds of life seemed to thrive—including mine. It was here that I was always safe.

Then the unthinkable happened. A firestorm struck down this magnificent place.

Many months passed before I was able to gather enough courage to ride back and survey my special haven. I was horrified. The devastation was so complete, so final. Nothing but charred blackness existed in this once spectacular place. My mighty oaks were gone. In their place remained only yawning cavernous holes where their roots had once been. They had been destroyed down to their very foundations.

I was completely overwhelmed as I slid off Firefly's back and walked through the sooty black powder. My tears broke through my emotional dam in an uncontrollable flood. This was my special place, my healing chamber, my home. Now it was destroyed beyond recognition. "Dear Jesus, this is just like my life," I sobbed.

The puffy, black soot billowed up nearly to my waist. Firefly and I had been walking a while, and finally my racking sobs subsided into silent tears that streamed down my face. And then I saw it. In the vast expanse of black one tiny oasis of color survived. I moved closer and knelt down to inspect this tiny pink wonder. A little plant had risen through the ash and, defying all the odds, dared to bloom in this world of black. Then I heard within my heart the unmistakable voice of the One who had knelt beside me so many years before. "You are right, child—this is just like your life. You see, I have raised you out of the ashes."

The truth of that moment has become even more powerful over time. A childhood event that should have destroyed my life instead, by Jesus' love, gave me life. I once had a horse that gave me refuge and saved my life. Now I have twenty-five that save other children's lives. I once lived in an ashen place. Now I live in an earthly paradise where by the grace of God I am allowed to be a steppingstone for others to leave their ashes behind. Life is so good, every moment so rich....

"Kim." The woman's voice on the phone yanked me back to the present. "Can you help?"

The little girl's mother and two brothers had been killed in an automobile accident. Her grief was so complete that she didn't seem to fully understand where she was, nor did it seem to matter. Her heart was in a cold, gray vortex of agony, sorrow, and loneliness. *I know that place,* I thought. And silently I prayed, *Lord, help me to be what this child needs.*

Friends of the family brought Madeline to the ranch. I helped her mount up in the round pen on a tall gray Anglo-Arab mare we had named Misha.

They'll make a good match, I thought. The horse had been named after Meshach, a young man in the Bible whom God had saved from a fiery furnace. A local rendering plant had been dispatched to send butchers to come and pick up the horse, but when they saw her emaciated condition they laughed and told the owner that she wasn't worth their time. I bought her shortly afterward. After gaining 380 pounds in our care, Misha was healthy, happy, and completely yielding to my simple voice commands. This bright filly had also left her ashes behind.

At first Madeline was tentative and unsure. Her thoughts were too fractured to allow her to focus. Her eyes stared straight down, and she held onto the saddle with both hands. From the middle of the round pen I gently commanded the horse. Misha seemed to recognize the child's sorrow and responded with such balanced tenderness that the girl would have needed no saddle at all.

After walking many patterned circles, Madeline seemed to relax a little. I decided that the concentration it would take for her to trot would be a simple distraction from her grief. After sharing with Madeline what to expect and how to move with the horse, I gently commanded Misha to trot. The young mare's body language conveyed that she understood she was carrying a very fragile child. By extending her head forward and down, she moved as if she were traveling over eggshells.

From time to time, Madeline looked in my direction and nodded at my instructions. Several times I saw her wavering hand leave the safety of the saddle horn and touch Misha's neck. It was a tiny step in a positive direction.

She continued to ride. I continued to pray.

Before our time was over, Madeline conveyed to me that she wanted to try cantering. It's not something I would normally allow, but I felt that this was an exceptional circumstance. I spent several moments instructing her, gently molding her fingers on the reins and adjusting the angles of her knees and ankles. Finally I asked Madeline if she was ready. She met my eyes and nodded.

Misha responded to my voice by reaching out with her forelegs in a smooth lope. I watched as the fluid rhythm unfolded before me—horse and rider moving as one—hair, mane, and tail waving in timeless unison. Around and around and around they cantered. Together their beauty circled me like a carousel.

Then quite suddenly the moment broke. It was time for the friends who had brought Madeline to go. She dismounted and left as quietly as she had come. Saddened by their quick departure, I wondered as I tacked down my gray "angel," *Was it enough, Lord? Did I do all I could to make an environment that would help bring healing?*

A short time later, Madeline moved away to live with her remaining family. I thought of her often, always with a twinge of sadness. I felt like I had failed to relieve this child's pain, to give her the safe and loving refuge that had been given to me.

Several weeks passed and I was standing in the checkout line at a local supermarket, thumbing through a batch of newly developed photographs. Suddenly I stopped. Somehow I had missed it. But now here it was, a moment captured in time—a photograph of Madeline cantering on Misha that day at the ranch. Both of Madeline's hands were gripping the pommel of the saddle. The gray filly's mane nearly covered them as it flowed back in the breeze. The girl's hair was floating freely behind her as well. Her chin was raised; her lips were parted in a soft smile. In the protective circle of our round pen, a brokenhearted little girl had left her pain behind just long enough to let a blissful smile find her lips.

But what moved me the most were her eyes…they were closed. And then I knew. I knew that for a brief moment, Madeline had truly found her refuge.

Maiden Voyage

WHEREVER SHE goes her white cane precedes her, gently tapping the ground with the rhythm of a metronome. Shelley is blind. I watched with fascination as step by measured step she explored the ranch. I couldn't help but wonder what it must be like, how hard it would be to understand a world you could not see.

Today was to be her maiden voyage—her first ride. We chose a young horse named River to carry her. He was a small bay Arabian gelding who was frightened of nothing. His easygoing personality resembled more that of a seasoned twenty-year-old than his scant four years. I felt that his kind and relaxed manner would suit Shelley well.

Under the gentle guidance of Elishah and Rachel, two of our senior staff, Shelley led River into the arena. She was helped off the top step of the mounting block and into the saddle. Before River began to move, Shelley asked with simple innocence, "What does it feel like to ride?"

Elishah and Rachel pondered her question for a moment before wisely returning with, "Why don't you tell us?" With that they began to lead River around the arena. The leaders watched with deep satisfaction as pure wonder began to shape the blind girl's expression.

In silence the little team walked nearly an entire lap before Shelley spoke. Her eyes fluttered closed and she tipped her chin upward as if trying to catch the breeze on her cheeks. "I can tell that I am really high up in the air," she finally said in a soft voice rich with imagination. Her eyes remained closed. "It's very windy up here. I feel like I could fly. Yes, if I put my wings out and fly, I can feel all of my troubles blowing away."

A Red Letter Day

❧

ARRY'S ILLNESS had advanced beyond medical control. Should he choose length of life and the agony-filled days that went with it or let nature lead the way to a shorter life of peace and dignity? Sorrow and peace, light and dark, pain and release—all were bound together in a whirlpool of emotion.

His decision was made. No more treatments, no more therapies. Harry's emotional storm subsided. But with that decision came great sacrifice. Harry fully understood that choosing to reject agonizing treatment for his illness would be more comfortable physically but also would cost him dearly in lost time with his family. When he crossed the finish line of his life, would anyone applaud his legacy? Was the life he was soon to leave behind prepared with enough love to carry his family through his absence? Who would comfort his loved ones in his place?

At the rich age of seventy-four, he was a devoted Missouri husband, father, and grandfather. But his family was scattered across the country, far from his arms like brilliant leaves swirling in a gusty fall wind. To travel across America's vast expanse to again hold his family in his arms would, like the fall leaves, become a thing of the past. It would soon be too painful and exhausting for him to endure. With a whispered prayer he determined that every cherished family moment would be a precious source of light and love in each of his remaining days.

God heard Harry's prayer.

I love my job because it allows me the honor of working with some of the dearest friends that the Lord has brought into my life. Among them is a couple, David and Petra, special friends whom I coach in strength training. They are close enough to speak truth into my life when I need help. Often, when I don't have the answers, their wisdom and love have become the banks of my river. They are counselors, working together to gently comfort and restore broken families.

As in most deeply rooted friendships, we had a foundational understanding of each other's families. I had been greatly saddened to hear that David's father, Harry, was dying of cancer.

One brisk February day David, Petra, and I were training together and talking about Harry's illness when a call for help came in to rescue a number of starving horses. Very few of the horses we rescue are donated; most of the time we must purchase their release—such was this case.

David and Petra responded immediately. By combining their finances with ours and some other caring friends', we were able to purchase the freedom of five two-year-old Arab colts. Once they were safely moved to the quarantine paddock that we keep for new arrivals, David and Petra came without delay to see them.

The young colts huddled together, their tiny bodies gaining courage from each other as they greeted us with their huge liquid brown eyes. No one spoke. I directed David's and Petra's attention to the weakest of them, a small bay colt at the back of the herd. Angular and gaunt, he looked to be in the worst condition. Even his heavy winter coat could not hide his ribs—they stood out like pickets in a fence.

From a distance, David stood and looked at the starving waif. For long minutes there was no movement other than the tousling of David's hair in the chilling wind. Even that could not penetrate the warmth that was growing between David and the colt. Almost imperceptibly the corners of David's mouth began to rise. The age-old union of man and horse drew them together. In those silent moments the needy colt moved into David's heart and became his adopted son.

For a time I watched in silence, not wanting to interrupt their unspoken communication. At last I spoke softly to David. "He needs a name." We made our way over to the young colt, working carefully through the massed bodies of the other youngsters. My friends began the bonding process of gently stroking him all over his deep red hide. David and Petra spoke softly between themselves, and in a few moments it was settled. "I'd like to name him 'Harry Leslie,'" David said, "in honor of my father." He grinned, stroking the horse's neck. "But we'll call him 'Tal.' That's my dad's nickname."

Eight months later, Troy and I were trying desperately to get out of town for a few badly needed days off. We had hoped to leave on Thursday. Already it was Saturday afternoon, and we were no closer to our goal. I was on the phone trying to finish up my list of calls. Troy was spinning around the living room like one of our own whirlwinds with travel bags, food, and camping gear.

Our dogs noisily announced someone's arrival. I heard Troy call out to David and Petra. His expression was puzzled as he walked out the door.

I was halfway down the hill when I saw that they had brought others with them. A well-built, iron-haired woman towing a little girl and a man I knew only through his son's descriptions. It was Harry Leslie. David had brought out his parents and his daughter.

Harry's pale complexion was completely overshadowed by the overwhelming warmth that radiated from his gentle eyes. Standing before Harry and his son, meeting their gazes, was like standing before a wood-burning stove on a brisk day. Their warmth drew you in, and the comfort spread over your heart like a sunrise. Even before I could release Harry's handshake, I knew that I loved him, just as I loved his son and daughter-in-law.

Troy brought out the colt, Tal, who by now had gained a hundred and fifteen pounds and had grown three inches taller. He tied him to the hitching post, where all of us pitched in to groom him. All but Harry Leslie. He stood a few feet away. I watched him intently, but his expression was difficult to read. While his son's family gathered around the young horse, Harry simply gazed at his name-sake. His eyes were so soft. Harry's brown eyes held the colt's brown eyes, unspoken communication pulled them together like a magnet. Slowly, without a word, Harry gently reached out with one finger toward the velvet muzzle that was reaching out toward him. They touched.

In that moment, only the Lord knows what transpired in their hearts. I looked on while man and beast united with each other, old and young meeting in a symbolic embrace. A gentle, older man passing on his strength, wisdom, and love to a young, green colt. Harry's eyes seemed to say, *Keep my memory alive, young one. Please love my family with all your heart. Grow up strong; catch their tears for me. Take good care of them, Tal.* Behind my sunglasses, deep within my heart, I could see the torch being passed.

David led Tal into the round pen to show Harry how beautifully the colt moved and to show him the ways in which horses communicate with people. Harry was completely captured! This was something he had only read about. Harry's granddaughter, Olivia, played about his feet, throwing sticks for the dogs to fetch. Then the little clouds of dust from Tal's hooves captured her attention, and she climbed up on the gate to see the horse as he cantered by.

Suddenly, it was as if someone had thrown a brick out of heaven. It landed squarely on top of my head. I knew exactly what I had to do.

Harry would never see this colt again. This was a moment he desperately needed to witness. He needed to see the circle completed. To know that young Tal would indeed carry on his torch, it was essential for him to see his granddaughter on Tal's back. I jogged across the yard to the tack room to collect a saddle and bridle. "Today is the day!" I declared, even though I knew that Tal had scarcely been used to a halter. Certainly he had never seen a saddle.

I carried the tack into the center of the round pen and allowed the colt to investigate the strange new items. Just like his namesake, Harry, in the face of the unknown, Tal was courageous. He seemed to understand how important this was. He was so kind and so willing. In a process that takes some horses weeks, Tal accepted the saddle and bridle in less than half an hour and was moving in a relaxed manner.

As utterly ridiculous as it seemed, I knew this was the right thing to do. *Lord, this is Your idea—make it become what it needs to be,* I prayed. We lifted Harry's five-year-old grand-daughter into the saddle. With her helmet in place and Mom and Dad on either side, we all stood ready for this first ride.

First one step, then another. I led Tal in a wide circle. The colt was totally at ease. He made lap after lap, and Olivia waved at her grandpa every time we passed the gate where Harry stood. I could see his eyes brimming with tears.

Tal seemed to understand what needed to happen. I'm sure that on one of our jubilant, waving circles he winked at Harry as he went by the gate—just to let him know that he knew what his name meant, and that the torch had truly been passed.

After many hugs, kisses, and carrots, we put Tal—the young "Harry Leslie"—away, returning him to a life where his only concerns were when to nap and who to play with next. His formal training would not come for another year. But I believe his life's calling was completed in that single day.

I heard later that when the family drove home, the car was filled with excited chatter, everyone talking at once about what they had all just witnessed.

As for Harry himself, he watched the farmland blur past the windows and was heard to softly repeat several times, "It was a red letter day. A red letter day...." When the chatter around him subsided, Harry said reflectively,

"I have had only three red letter days in my life. Today was one of them."

A fact more certain than our life is our death—it comes to us all. It is within our life now while we live that we must prepare the gifts, the baton that we will pass on. What is worthy to be passed on? What is not? Which are we spending the most time on?

Little things do count. I doubt that when David and Petra generously bought the salvation of a desperate colt, they realized they were freeing the hearts of two captives—a young dying horse and an old dying man. Who can know the path that kindness may travel?

What were Harry Leslie's two other red letter days? We never knew. But who could have known the third would come dressed in three white socks and a star on his forehead?

The Silent Meeting

THE BEAUTIFUL spring day was already blooming with possibilities. A midmorning breeze carried with it the light sage fragrance of the high desert. It felt like perfumed satin on my arms and face.

I had arranged for an informal meeting at the ranch with the leaders of some of our community service groups. We decided to hold it upstairs in our unfinished barn, where there were no walls or roof to separate us from the outdoors.

During our meeting, several vanloads of kids arrived. They were with an organization that helps meet the needs of children from extremely low-income homes. Although I had seen many of these youngsters before, I noticed a few new faces in the crowd. Despite the meeting in progress, five of the junior-high girls crept up the barn stairs. They surrounded me; two sat on each side of my bench seat, while the fifth girl sat cross-legged on the floor between my knees.

I greeted each girl with a silent touch as the meeting went on over their heads. The girl on the floor, resting her head on my knee, played with the laces of my boots. I began to rub her head and finger-comb her hair.

The girl on my far right was a child I hadn't seen

before. She had brown hair and dark eyes set in an exotic mocha toned face. Even in her disheveled state, she was a stunning beauty. With intense, intelligent eyes she watched my every move like a bird of prey. Her eyes traveled from my fingers, which were now methodically braiding hair, to my face, and back to my hands again.

I finished braiding the seated girl's hair. Without taking my eyes off the man who was addressing the meeting, I leaned forward and whispered to the girl to hold the end of her braid while she went to the tack room to find a couple of rubber bands.

She stood quietly, careful to stay low so that she wouldn't cause a disturbance. The instant her foot left the space between my boots, the girl on my left jumped down into her place. I began to finger-comb, as best as I could, her wild tousle of blond hair.

The scrutiny from the girl on my right continued uninterrupted. Out of the corner of my eye, I could see her gaze on my face. Then her eyes dropped back down to my hands, watching hungrily as I wove the blond girl's hair into an elegant queen's crown braid.

The little blonde, inspecting her coiffure with her hands, followed the first girl out of the loft. Like the falling of a domino, the child on my immediate right quickly fell into place. She had long, dark hair that hung in filthy clumps around her small head. *Oh well,* I thought, *hands can be washed.* I plunged in, separating her oily locks, and noticed that my little coffee-colored spy was now including the newly vacated space between us in her searching gaze.

The next time she looked at my face, I turned and smiled directly at her. Her black eyebrows drew together, as though she were trying to understand a foreign language. Still smiling, I returned to the greasy braid growing in my hands.

Now she wasn't looking at my face or hands at all. She studied only the empty space on the bench between us. I could feel tension rising like a static charge—a tension brought on by the immense conflict building within her heart. Anxiety produced an adrenaline flush that made her skin glow auburn, like a harvest sunset. Moments passed as she stared at the space between us. I could literally feel her immense conflict; something big was building within her.

At last with silent, profound courage, she did it. Inch by inch, as innocent as falling snow and with half the speed, she began to slide toward me. Still focused only on the space left between us, she watched it until it vanished and the outside of our thighs touched.

Her gaze remained low as if she were flying under radar and trying to delay being detected. Now her body was perfectly still. She acted like a child on thin ice, afraid that any movement would fracture this fragile place, plunging her into cold darkness. Suddenly it made sense—this child lived outside the light of love. For her, affection *was* a foreign language. She wanted desperately to be loved like the other girls but didn't know how to ask.

The adults continued to ramble on. More girls had crept into the meeting to join us. My dark little beauty watched them with lowered eyes. I finished the oily fishtail braid, and another girl with very short blond hair immediately slid into the vacated place at my feet. I began to knead her tiny back and shoulders. Sadly I sensed the anxiety rising again on my right. Her small frame stiffened.

Could the need for acceptance and love generate this much turmoil? No child, I resolved, *should suffer like this.* Without taking my hands from the blond girl's shoulders, I simply turned to the right and gave my dark-eyed lamb a kiss on the top of her head.

She sat rigid and still for the longest moment. Until finally, with a heave of her entire body, she released an enormous sigh. I smiled to myself.

The leaders of the meeting kept on talking around us. Occasionally I joined in. Squealing laughter and the shuffling of hooves on woodchips rose through the floor below us as the kids began to groom and tack up the horses.

Still gently kneading the tiny back between my knees, I looked to the girl still tentatively pressed against my right leg. Finally she looked back up at me. Her eyes were huge with uncertainty. They seemed to ask, "Are you going to make me leave now?"

I answered her with a smile and a wink. She stared at me, expressionless, and then her chin dropped and she slouched back into contemplation again.

Time passed. And then rather suddenly she sat up straight. With stealth, her dark eyes slid to the left and focused on my shoulder with the concentration of a marksman pinpointing his target. Her blazing intensity could have raised a blister on my bare skin.

I watched her with puzzled amusement. Overpowering her body's inhibitions with sheer will power, she made her move. With the awkward, incremental movements of a robot, she clicked her neck sideways until her ear lightly touched my shoulder.

It looked right, but it wasn't. Her body was in the

correct position but her confidence wasn't—it was in a fierce battle to survive. This remarkable triumph could have passed unnoticed, but it didn't. Without a word, I slipped my right arm behind her and firmly enfolded her against my side. With just my fingertips I traced little patterns up and down her arm and across her back, alternately rubbing her petite neck and combing her beautiful hair.

As before, she finally exhaled with a mighty effort. Her bones seemed to flow out with her released breath as she completely crumpled against me.

My heart was as full as the breezy outdoors blowing around us. Adult voices rose and fell over our heads in harmony with the wind in the pines as the meeting continued. Yet another meeting, a silent meeting, drew to a warm conclusion as a newly converted snuggle-bug nestled under my right arm.

hope
rising
above
pain

Wings to Fly

⟨flourish⟩

OUR FIRST introduction came on an exceptionally warm September day. I looked down to see a shy eight-year-old girl with tangled blond hair peeking around her mother's leg. She stood with her arms either behind her back or hanging straight down at her sides. She was downcast, chin down, head down; only her eyes lifted briefly to look at me. They were beautiful, pale blue pools with dark rims—intense, intelligent, and profoundly sad.

Despite the warm weather, she wore a little vest decorated with horses. This little girl needed to be here. I knew she desperately needed acceptance by someone who would love her just as she was. "What's your name?" I asked, crouching down to her level.

Without looking up, she simply replied, "Robin."

I complimented her on the beautiful vest she wore and asked, "Would you like to ride a horse?" Her response was a solemn nod.

Soon we were kneeling in front of a small, freckled mare, preparing to feed her some well-deserved carrots. I held Robin's tiny hands in mine and watched the wonder come over her face as the horse's soft muzzle touched her hands for the first time. In those moments, her eyes changed. The furrow between her blond eyebrows relaxed into a smooth, flawless plane. Her heart responded like snow to a spring thaw.

Together we groomed and tacked the gentle mare. I helped Robin snap on her helmet, and then she was ready for her first ride. She received her few simple instructions with the sobriety of a judge, but underneath I could sense a continuing thaw of her emotions. Droplets formed beneath the radiance of trust. Falling like tears, they converged into tiny rivulets. The small streams began to gather and swell into a rising current of confidence. In this moment of time she was allowing a horse to go where no one had been permitted for a long time. The carefully built walls of her heart were, step by step, being smashed beneath the hooves of a newfound trust.

The falling of the autumn leaves mirrored the falling away of Robin's self-consciousness. With the remarkable resilience of a child, her heart began to change as brick by brick a new foundation of hope was being constructed. Daily, her sense of confidence and self-esteem increased. She was a voracious student, learning at an exceptional rate, while her initial intensity was now being systematically eroded by frequent girlish giggles. Her laughter, now lacking its former anchor of fear, was increasingly finding its way to the surface.

On a chilly fall day I watched in amazement as Robin cantered by. I had to remind myself that she had been riding for only a few weeks. Toward the end of her lesson, I joined her mother at the arena rail for no other reason than to share how impressed I was by Robin's riding ability. I had just begun to speak when I saw her mother's eyes rapidly filling with tears. Her diminutive frame began to shake, and she covered her mouth with one tiny hand. With her other she cradled her infant son. Her huge eyes closed tightly for a moment.

The only sound was that of her other young daughter who was nearby throwing sticks for our puppy. Time seemed to hold its breath. At last, Robin's mother turned to me and said softly, "If we hadn't found this place, we would have lost her." Her tears fell in silence as together we watched Robin in the arena, stride by stride, leave her demons behind.

Robin's journey toward self-confidence continued, and one week before Thanksgiving I watched this precious blond girl with no help at all, ride a tall, elegant Anglo-Arab mare. The mare's graceful mane and tail and Robin's ponytail all combined in a floating rhythm under the brilliant evening sky. Set against a deep purple and magenta horizon, it was like watching a dance, human and equine hearts moving together in a timeless embrace.

I bit my gloves off and clapped my bare, cold hands together so she could hear me. She trotted in toward me, and I spread my arms wide open and shouted, "Wow!" Reaching up, balancing on my tiptoes, I met her in a huge hug. Her little face glowed. She was not the same girl I had met only seven weeks before. "I'm so proud of you, Robin. I know your parents are, too," I added, as she prepared to cool the horse down. "Your dad would be amazed to see what you've done here. When are you going to invite him to come and watch you?"

Her glow quickly faded into shades of gray. Her eyes dropped to the ground. "He'll never come," she finally said in a quiet voice. "He's too busy."

The grip of poverty had pushed this young family

nearly to the breaking point. I could only imagine a young father of three trying to maintain the balance between work and family. Clearly, from this eight-year-old's perspective, Dad was absent from the things that she valued the most.

We rushed to tack down under the final applause of what had been a violently beautiful sunset. *What a remarkable end to a spectacular day,* I thought, as I watched this precious family drive down the hill and away from the ranch.

Suddenly, in the twilight, bright red taillights flashed. Before the car had completely stopped, the passenger door opened, and a small, familiar form came running back to me. "I almost forgot," Robin puffed. "I have something for you." Her little clutched hand rose toward my face, and in the dim light I could see that she was holding a tiny school picture of herself.

"Honey, you are so beautiful!" I exclaimed as I turned the picture over. What I read on the back dropped me to my knees. My voice nearly failed as I tried to thank her. From my knees, I wrapped my arms around her tiny body and hugged her tightly.

Still kneeling in the dust after they had driven away, I looked again at my little picture. Next to a childlike drawing of a horse, the inscription said simply, "Thank you for giving me wings so I can fly."

Pony of Gold

A SOLITARY PONY stood with his tail turned toward the bitter November wind. From birth this animal was meant to be surrounded by his own kind, to be part of a herd, to be part of a family—but he stood alone. His long, ragged coat did little to hide his bony frame. The pony was old, past his prime, his usefulness all but gone.

In the wake of the setting sun, waves of gray blanketed the earth. As darkness fell, the temperature dropped with it. The wind carried the scent of snow.

When ponies look into the night sky, do they dare to ponder? Do they hope to be loved by someone special? Do they wish to become a child's dream come true?

After deep consideration and prayer, I felt that it was time to make the call. Robin's mother was silent as I shared my idea. "What do you think?" I finally asked.

After a small hesitation she seemed to find her voice. "I think it's wonderful. It's every little girl's dream to have a horse of her own."

We decided we would begin looking for a horse for Robin, both agreeing that, if it were meant to be, the money would arrive for the purchase of the horse and its continued care at our ranch. "Do you believe in miracles?" I asked.

With thoughtful deliberation, she replied with a quiet yes. I smiled. "So do I." The wheels of prayer were set in motion.

Miracles fill the space that is given to them. They can be as small as a twinkle or larger than the midnight sky. However, unlike dreams, miracles come to life. They are powered by the smile of an Almighty God and profoundly change all who are touched by them. Many have said, "Seeing is believing," when in reality just the opposite is true: "*Believing* is seeing."

Several days later I stood at the counter of the local feed store, preparing to carry out my purchase. I had told the store manager about Robin and asked if he might know of anyone who had a suitable horse for her. Across the counter the rancher's warm, weathered face spread into an easy smile. "I believe I have her horse," he grinned beneath his moustache.

The anticipation of seeing this little horse made my heart do somersaults! *Is he the one?* I wondered. Troy and I made the long trip to the rancher's home, and the information that he had given me kept swirling around in my mind. The little horse was older, a buckskin Pony of America, recently purchased from a dude string that had gone out of business. The pony had been carelessly cast aside and would probably have met an unfortunate end if the rancher hadn't intervened.

We rounded a long bend in the road, and I could see him in the distance. He stood alone in a barren field. His lowered head and expression were so somber. He stood very still, like a crumbling statue long forgotten in a world of stone.

When we approached, a particularly strong gust of bitter cold wind visibly rolled through the field, swirling debris violently around him. I don't know if it was the wind or the hope of being loved again, but something inside him suddenly came to life. His humble head and tail snapped up, and he met us near the gate at a full gallop.

At the hitching post, I finally had a chance to touch him. I ran my hands across his cheek, along his neck, and down his side. An immediate wave of sorrow rose from my stomach and tightened my throat. He was desperately thin. "Poor little man," I whispered. His winter coat was so long that I didn't see his miserable condition at first, but now I could not look away. Without special care, this golden pony might not be able to withstand the brutality of a Central Oregon winter.

Gently, I began to massage his thin back. He cautiously turned to look at me. His expression was hesitant, unsure and questioning. We gazed at each other for a moment before I realized that this forsaken little soul had probably never been touched in this way. Perhaps he had never been anyone's pet, only someone's property.

"What's his name?" I asked the rancher without looking up. I was caught off guard by his answer, an answer that brought unexpected tears to my eyes. It portrayed the exact image I'd had of Robin the last time I watched her ride.

"His name is...Dancer."

Without knowing more, my mind was made up. It felt as if the last puzzle piece had been fitted into place and the picture had suddenly become clear. I decided to do whatever it took to save this old, starving, golden pony for a young, starving, golden-haired girl.

"Five hundred dollars is his price," the rancher said over my shoulder.

"Hmm," I mumbled, turning to look at him. "I don't have five hundred dollars, but I know that if this is the good Lord's idea, the money will come."

As only a cowboy can, his slow smile embodied all the warmth of a lazy summer afternoon. On this bitter cold night, it seemed to warm the space between us. He extended his calloused hand, and we shook in strong agreement.

Dusk had slipped into dark as we turned our old pickup toward home. I couldn't help but wonder what the future would hold for this pony. I looked up into the starry winter night, and a simple child's prayer left my heart and followed my gaze up into the heavens.

The following day bustled with activity on the ranch. Parents and their children scrambled about preparing costumes for the participants and their horses for the following Saturday's Christmas parade. I stood in the arena blowing warmth into my hands. I enjoyed being surrounded by the happy sights and sounds of utter chaos as my young riders prepared for their big day. Cold wind whipped glittering tinsel in all directions. The dark sky overhead and the very air around me came to life with the sound of literally hundreds of jingle bells carefully fastened to our patient horses.

My chaotic bliss was interrupted when, with the gentleness of a dove, tiny arms wrapped around my waist. A beleaguered little cherub looked up at me and smiled. I bent down and kissed the top of her head. I looked down into Robin's deep twin pools of blue. Her eyes were so large in her tiny, rosy-cheeked face. I could feel the sun rise within my heart. I straightened and looked up to see...her dad!

His gaze was lost in the confusion of the merry crowd around us. He looked a bit like a deer in headlights, torn between facing the onslaught or fleeing to safety. I made my way across the arena and intercepted him with a big smile and a handshake. Although his eyes moved like ricocheting bullets, he seemed to calm a little with our light conversation. Still his behavior suggested that of someone tied down on a railroad track—and the train was coming.

The whirlwind of people, horses, and decorations swirled throughout the afternoon. I sought out Robin's dad as often as time would allow and talked to him about the upcoming parade, the ranch, his kids, and the golden pony that I had found the day before. He listened carefully and offered polite questions but was otherwise very quiet.

When I hugged his young family good-bye, I still wasn't sure how he interpreted the day, our ranch, or me. It saddened me to think that none of it had made a very good impression in all of the confusion of the afternoon.

Later that evening I called the young family to wrap up a few details concerning the parade. Robin's mother answered in her soft-spoken voice. Upon hearing it was me, she moved to a private location in their house and told me something totally unexpected. "I'm not sure what happened at the ranch today, but when my husband came home, he went into our bedroom and just sat down on the bed. When I asked him what was wrong, he told me about the pony that you had talked to him about. Kim, he told me that he would like nothing more than to buy that pony for our children. Unfortunately we are so broke right now that nothing outside of a miracle would make it possible. But he continued to talk about the kids and the pony for a while. This has obviously had a big impact on him."

I was left to ponder this new information. From my perspective, the young father seemed removed and uncomfortable. Yet for him, the reality of the day had apparently pierced his heart like an arrow. I couldn't help but hope that an event like this, acquiring a pony for Robin, would bring together their struggling hearts.

In a single day the dream turned into a living miracle. Seven different people, only one of whom knew about the pony, donated nearly to the penny the purchase price of the little horse!

Troy and I wasted no time and drove out that night to purchase the pony. It was the eve of Thanksgiving. The wind was driving a light snow into our trailer when the pony jumped into the black space without hesitation.

"Does the kid have her own tack?" the rancher asked, tipping his head to the side so his cowboy hat would block the falling snow.

"No, nothing," I replied.

"That's no good," he said over his shoulder as he walked into the blackness of his barn. He returned carrying two small, well-used saddles. "A kid's gotta' have her own gear. Either of these outta' do," he said with his trademark smile. "My boys've grown outta them; no reason they shouldn't work for her." And he laid a saddle over each of my arms.

After a thankful hug and a kiss to the rancher, Troy and I made our way home, pulling behind us a very remarkable gift. Snowflakes blurred in and out of our headlight beams, and I couldn't help but feel that each one represented a special blessing in my life. Hundreds of thousands of little gifts, each unique and different, each adding to the unmistakable foundation of joy in my heart. *Yes, Lord, I have so much to be thankful for.*

"Who is this?" Robin asked, her wide blue eyes peering at me through her tousled blond hair.

My answer was nonchalant. "He's a pony that needed a new home."

She stroked him tenderly, then tilted her head up at me and thoughtfully asked, "Can I ride him?"

"Sure," I said, turning away. I didn't trust my expression to conceal our secret.

Following a light ride and much grooming, we placed a special pan of feed for the pony on the picnic table. While he ate, Robin lay limp in the curve of his back, her arms and legs draped on either side. Her blond head was cradled in his heavy black mane. She was facing away from us as her mother and I approached, and we stumbled into her private conversation.

"You are the most beautiful pony I have ever seen," Robin whispered. "I hope that someday I can have a pony just like you. I love you, Dancer," she added, while trying to hug his neck. From somewhere above, I know angels smiled. I silently reached for her mother's hand and together we quietly walked back to the barn.

"Hello," Robin's father answered amid squealing children. He and I chatted briefly, and then I told him we needed privacy and to go into the bedroom and close the door.

"I have something I need to tell you," I began. "Do you remember when I told you about the golden pony?"

"Yes," he answered quietly.

"Do you remember when I said that if God was in it, He would provide for it?"

"Yes," he said, more as a question than an answer.

Not wanting to leave him in suspense, I forged ahead. "I want you to know that your wife, children, and I have been praying. I'm calling to tell you that something remarkable has happened." I heard only silence.

I could only imagine, after an introduction like that, what must have been going through his mind. I continued. "Within one day of our last conversation, seven people donated enough money for us to buy the golden pony." More silence. "The pony is safe and now living on our ranch. I'm calling to tell you that we have purchased the pony solely to give to you...so you can give him to Robin for Christmas."

This time, I waited for a reply.

When his voice finally came through, it was choked with emotion. "Why...why are you doing this for me? You don't even know me; why are you doing this? I'm not sure what to say...."

"I'm doing this for you because long ago someone did it for me, and my life was saved because of it. Maybe someday you will have a chance to do something like this for someone else. That's how this works, you know," I said in a soft voice. My imagination pictured him sitting on the edge of the bed with his head in his hands as silent tears fell to the floor.

Finally, in a weak voice, he managed to say, "Thank you."

Christmas morning dawned, crackling with expectation. The air was crisp with winter's grasp. Our plans had been laid before the family drove up our hill. Robin, having been led to think that she was bringing me gifts for the ranch, joyfully presented me with a hoof pick, a little brush, and a tiny red saddle pad. I knelt among the children and gave them all hugs. While I was still holding them, their father led from the barn a beautifully groomed pony dressed in red garlands. A note was tied around his neck with red ribbons. The children all looked up at the pony with bewilderment. They honestly didn't know what was happening. "Hurry, go read the note!" their mother prompted Robin with excitement.

Carefully she opened the note. Immediately, her little blond head shot up to look at her dad's face, then at the pony, then at her mother. Without words she was asking, "Is this true?"

With a deep smile, her father finally said, with a nod, "He's yours."

Disbelief quickly melted into a huge astonished smile. If hugs and kisses for Dancer had been snowflakes, he would have been buried beneath their blizzard.

At last Robin nestled her tear-streaked face into the

soft golden curve of Dancer's neck, small fingers clutching tight little handfuls of his long coat. It was a gesture that seemed to proclaim, "I'll never let you go."

I looked into the pony's face and I wondered: As Robin had been dreaming of him, had he been dreaming of her? Wasn't this what every horse desired—to be the sun in a child's sky? Isn't it everyone's dream to be loved, without conditions attached, every day of their life?

Before, he was nothing more than a golden pony. A crumbling little soul left to stand abandoned on a desolate hill. By the power alone of a child's love, he was transformed into a priceless pony of gold.

It's Good

THEIR VAN WAS the first to make tracks in the freshly fallen snow on the ranch's common area. The air was still rich with its distinct cold fragrance. Gray mist began to settle around us as a mother, a therapist, and I gathered around the van door to receive the child waiting inside.

I had talked with the mother before their visit and learned that Jamie couldn't speak, nor could she walk without assistance. Her physical movements were jerky and exaggerated. Her fine motor skills appeared only in random bursts, like the taps and bars of a Morse code message. Bacterial meningitis had attacked her central nervous system. By her seventh day of life, the frontal lobes of her brain had been destroyed, she was on oxygen, and in constant seizures. The doctors quietly prepared Jamie's parents for her death.

I understood that Jamie spent nearly her first year of life in the hospital and survived eighteen surgeries. I asked her mother how she did it; how did she keep her emotions from spinning into a shattered mess? With simple wisdom she said, "I had to just keep reminding myself that God loves her more than I do. Through the darkest times, that was enough."

I peeked into the van and gave Jamie a wide smile.

This was our first meeting, and her eyes locked searchingly onto my face. Her bewildered look confirmed that she didn't know or recognize me.

A special belt with handles was fitted around Jamie's waist, so that others could assist her. Simply getting out of the van was an enormously difficult task for her. But her face was bright, and my heart received a powerful lesson from this struggling eleven-year-old as clearly as if she had been able to speak the words: Life is good.

Through the mist, I led out one of our Arab geldings, a gray named Lightfoot. Like Jamie, he, too, had a triumphant spirit. We had rescued him years ago from a desperate situation. He had been forced to live by eating straw and as a result developed a life-threatening intestinal impaction. We had found him on a snowy evening like this one, lying on the ground. His limbs were rigid with agonizing pain as he thrashed in the terminal stages of colic. After many days of intensive care, he not only survived certain death but soared beyond it to become a top ten endurance racing horse.

I thought Lightfoot would be a good match for Jamie. With all that they both had overcome in their lives, I was certain they would relate to each other on a level beyond my understanding.

At the hitching post, our little team gathered around the gelding. Ami, one of my dedicated senior staff, was helping, along with Jamie's therapist. With our hands over Jamie's, we manipulated her into holding a brush so that she could groom Lightfoot's damp winter coat. She allowed us to puppet her movements through the whole process until the horse was tacked up and ready to ride.

I wasn't sure how much Jamie understood of what she

had just accomplished or of what was about to happen. I wanted so much for her to comprehend that this was a kind, living creature willing to share some special time with her. We all moved into the arena, and I guided Jamie until she was standing directly in front of Lightfoot. She blinked up at what must have looked like huge nostrils. The gelding's misty breath billowed around her tiny form. Gently I stroked his upper lip.

Jamie seemed intrigued. I bent to kiss Lightfoot's soft muzzle. As I pulled back, the girl leaned in. Inch by inch, she drew closer to his velvety nose. His heavy streams of breath poured past her pink cheeks, enveloping her clothing in a damp silver gloss. She pursed her lips in a preformed kiss, nearly touching her nose to his. But then, instead of a peck on his upper lip, she slipped out the tip of her tongue and licked him! A simple kiss, it seemed, would not be good enough to explore this strange new surface! Lightfoot received her unusual caress with warm brown eyes.

All of us helped to lift Jamie into the saddle. Her face registered nothing but puzzlement. Ami led Lightfoot slowly around the arena, with the therapist balancing Jamie on one side and me on the other. Snow had started to fall again, great wet flakes that coated our heads and shoulders. Jamie's mother, heavily bundled up against the cold, stood watching by the arena rail.

We had just completed our second circuit around the arena when we heard a sudden strange sound over our muffled footsteps. I looked around. There it was again. Jamie's voice! For the first time in our presence, she was vocalizing!

Looking up at her through the falling snow, I saw that she had pushed her hands together and was bumping the horse's mane with them. Her face glowed with excitement, and with each bump of her hands she uttered an odd little "guh" sound.

Fascinated, we watched as an amazing scene unfolded before us. As Jamie's bumping became more insistent, her vocalizations grew louder and louder. Soon her whole body was adding emphasis to her exclamations. With each "guh" she lunged forward, driving her locked arms against the patient gelding's neck. None of us were quite certain what to make of this rousing display of intense emotion. We smiled at Jamie's rising enthusiasm but struggled to understand what she was trying to tell us.

"Do you like this?" I asked, smiling up at her. She turned toward the sound of my voice and, with her mouth wide open, revealed all of her teeth in an enormous beaming smile. I laughed out loud.

We rounded the top end of the arena, and as we approached the girl's mother again, each step seemed to inspire more eagerness in the brilliant-faced child. "Guh, guh, guh!" she nearly shouted.

"What is she saying?" I asked her mother when we were close enough.

She didn't answer. I looked across at her over Lightfoot's back to see if she had heard me. She had. Her face was streaming with tears; her hands were tightly clasped under her chin. She drew a deep breath and wiped her eyes. "She's telling you," she said, "'it's good. It's good. It's good!'"

Lord, Have Mercy

OTHING IN ALL my experience of rescuing horses could have prepared my heart for what I was facing. My legs literally gave way, and I dropped to my knees. How could anyone let this happen? Over and over the same thought kept finding its way to my numbed lips. *Lord, have mercy...Lord, have mercy.*

The whole scene was surreal. How was it possible to witness anything so devastating on such a glorious spring day? This was by far the most desperate case of neglect I had ever seen.

The shadow of a horse that stood before me was a seventeen-year-old gray mare. The exotic facial structure proclaiming her Arabian lineage still remained, but her eyes were deeply sunken. I could imagine the spirited fire that had once flashed within them, could see the proud carriage of that sculpted head, the arching of her well-muscled neck.... But now she was only a skeleton with skin, her muscles wasted to nothing more than sinew along bone. Her eyes revealed the dull glow of dying embers.

She made a brave attempt to come to me. Reaching out with one unsteady foreleg, she placed it carefully, testing her footing. Then she heaved her diminished weight over the leg to form a step. She paused, her head swaying from side to side, struggling desperately to hold her precarious balance. This simple movement—the taking of one step—caused her breath to come in shallow, labored gasps. Then she put her other front leg forward and, with extreme concentration, repeated the same process. The effort left her trembling, weaker than before, yet she stretched her face to me and her quivering lips touched my forehead. Kneeling beside her, I wept out loud.

What made the whole scene unfathomably worse was knowing that this pitiful skeleton of a mare was ten months pregnant. She was very close to death. My stomach clenched and churned as if it could reject what my eyes were seeing. I got back up to my feet and started to run. I cut through the owner's twenty-acre field to reach my truck as fast as possible, for once not caring that I was trespassing on private property. Time was running out.

I had not been invited to this property by the owners. The Sheriff's Department and the Humane Society had asked for my help in placing sixteen needy horses. At Crystal Peaks, even if we can't keep every horse in need, we rescue and rehabilitate them, and then find a place for them through a network we have developed of safe adoptive homes.

This mare needed help *now*.

I reached home and made the appropriate calls. In a whirlwind turnaround, I sped back to the place where Mercy, as we had now christened the mare, was dying. Angela, one of my staff, was with me, and we had our empty horse trailer in tow. My dear friends at the Redmond Veterinary Clinic had been alerted and were ready to receive the mare.

Angela and I carefully guided Mercy into the trailer as

several cars drove by, honking, waving, and giving thumbs-up approval to what we were doing. One woman actually stopped. She powered down the window of her pickup truck and yelled, "I'm so glad that you're taking her. I've had to drive by like this for the last year!" She held her hand up to the side of her face, as if to shield herself from having to see the starving mare.

I watched in complete bewilderment as the woman drove away. All of these people seemed to have known about Mercy's increasingly desperate condition. But as far as I knew, none of them had done anything to help her. They had stood casually by, watching the starving mare day by day as she slipped away.

Without a voice, how can a horse beg for mercy?

The fifty-five-minute trip back to the veterinary clinic seemed an eternity. "Lord, hold her up," I prayed, constantly looking back through the tinted windows of the trailer to see if the silhouette of the mare's ears was still visible.

At the clinic, we led Mercy one step at a time out of the trailer and into a treatment room. Shawn—a pillar of a friend—was the vet who came to attend the mare. Simultaneous anger, sorrow, and compassion vied for expression in his face. He glanced at me over Mercy's back, and even before he spoke I knew the worst from the deep furrows in his brow.

Yet as hopeless as the mare's condition seemed, Shawn worked on her, swiftly, with gentleness and care, as if he were treating a beloved child and not merely an abandoned horse. Once he had done all he could, he relayed what he had found. Her emaciated state had most likely caused her to sustain serious liver and kidney damage. Shawn doubted that she would be able to carry her foal to term simply because she wouldn't live long enough. We parted with sobriety on both sides. Medically, everything possible had been done. Time now for the dreaded "wait and see."

Like people, horses are sometimes their own worst enemies. We moved Mercy back to our ranch, but she wasn't comforted by her new surroundings. She wasted vital energy looking for a companion. We tried putting our old gentle pony in with her, but her monumental efforts to stand with him cost her too much. Time after time she stumbled to the ground. If only we could explain to her, "You need to be still." But we couldn't. We could only stand by and watch her struggle.

The next day was worse. Early morning light spread, pale gray, over the land—and over my heart. Mercy had spent a brutal night, falling down over and over, and then flailing about in her efforts to stand up again. Now she was down. Her skin had broken open in many places. Her own blood made startling patterns on her silvery white body. Her head and legs were stained with blood.

Angela, Troy, and I tried to comfort her. She was still struggling to stand, but her strength was rapidly failing. We knelt by her, trying to keep her calm and quiet, stroking her bruised and bleeding body.

That morning we were expecting a group of eight-year-old girls—Brownies who were coming to do volunteer work at the ranch. Troy left Mercy's side to intercept them and returned later with his cell phone in hand. It was Shawn.

I gave our vet a rundown of the mare's condition, and then in a broken voice I asked him to come. No living creature should suffer like this.

He quietly said, "I'm on my way."

I wiped my face and took several deep breaths before I strode over to the little group of Brownies. *Lord, help me to be wise,* I prayed.

"We have a horse that is very sick," I began, wiping my bloody hands on my jeans. "No one gave her the help that she needed to get well. Now she will never get well. She's dying." I heard my voice crack and pressed my blood-smeared hands to my face.

The girls were wide-eyed and silent. Finally, I looked up and suggested to the accompanying parents that the children ought to be allowed to see the mare. They needed to know what can happen when people don't take care of their animals. The parents agreed. The little procession made its way silently past the dying mare. Some of the girls walked by quickly, without looking up. Others stopped and stared. The adults, more aware of what was really happening, ushered the youngsters by without speaking.

The day had to go on. I set the Brownies to their tasks and then returned to Mercy.

In that short while, her condition had slipped considerably. She could no longer breathe lying on her side, but she was too weak to sit up on her knees. We had to roll her up onto her chest so that she could gasp a few breaths before collapsing back against our arms.

Every movement now was agonizing for her. Her lungs were beginning to fill with fluid. Blood flowed from her mouth and nostrils. Her fragile skin started to tear just from the pressure of our hands and legs as we tried to help her. Then her belly—the only part of her body not entirely shrunken because of the foal she still carried—began to jerk with violent spasms. Her foal was dying.

Her eyes now were staring, wide and dry, coated with debris because she no longer blinked. Her mortal struggle crescendoed into gruesome attempts to draw shallow, rattling breaths.

"Lord, have mercy," I sobbed over and over. "Lord, have mercy."

Shawn arrived.

I stood up to meet him as he crossed the yard, but I didn't get very far. He took in the blood on my hands and legs and after a quick assessment returned to the corral with a large syringe.

My tongue seemed to detach itself from my brain. Not wanting to accept what was about to happen, I stupidly asked, "Is this the right thing to do?"

Shawn nodded. He didn't need words to communicate what he, too, was feeling. His blue eyes turned into glassy pools as he knelt down beside Mercy and began to stroke her neck and shoulder. His assistant put her hand on my shoulder.

There wasn't anything to say.

Stroking the fine, proud contours of Mercy's bloodied head, I thought about the magnificent Arabian horse she once had been. If we had found her sooner, if we could have rescued her in time, what might have been?

I sobbed for what would never be. She would never again be brushed by gentle hands. Her silky white mane would never again glisten like spun pearls drifting under a golden sky. She would never prance with flaring nostrils and proudly arched neck, showing all the glory of her heritage. She would never know her foal. She would never feel love again.

It was time.

Shawn injected the mare. We could see the lethal fluid snaking from the needle into the vein in her neck. Her straining muscles relaxed, as though she were at last finding rest. Her indomitable will to live had been overcome.

Her eyes died first. She exhaled slowly as her head and neck crumpled into Angela's lap. All that remained of this once glorious purebred mare was her torn and bloody body. Angela sobbed as she cradled Mercy's head against her cheek.

Anguish erupted in my heart—a violent outpouring of sorrow rose up in my throat like scalding lava. I wanted to scream. I wanted the world to know that it had lost a magnificent creature. I wanted to throw my head back and let out all my futile rage.

In the distance I heard children laughing as they played. A gentle breeze moved through the tree over our heads. I closed my eyes and envisioned Mercy galloping with her face to the wind, her newborn foal at her side.

They were finally free.

Time slipped away. Together, Troy, Angela, and I covered Mercy's body with a tarp. It was spring, and I could find only three flowers blooming on the ranch. Daffodils. We placed them carefully on the dead mare's shoulder.

I was leaning heavily on the corral fence when I felt something hugging my thigh. An eight-year-old girl was looking up at me with enormous brown eyes. Her cheeks were smudged with tears. With the sweet innocence of a child, she said simply, "I'm sorry your horse died."

I knelt down to hug her and whispered into her hair, "Me, too."

Thinking back to my first moments with the mare the day before, I remembered praying through my torment, "Lord, have mercy."

My prayer had been answered. The good Lord is ultimately merciful. I asked Him to have "Mercy."

Now He does.

A Perfect Match

⟨∞⟩

*J*UST WALKING up the hill that leads to our ranch made Mary's breath come in shallow pants. Her skin was deathly pale, and a bluish cast covered her eyes and lips. During our simple greeting, it was very apparent that this woman was gravely ill.

Mary had come to Crystal Peaks from Washington State with her husband and two children. After we made our introductions, one of my staff quietly brought a chair so that Mary could sit down and catch her breath.

Although her body had been ravaged by illness, there was something remarkable, something indomitable about her spirit. Her expression, though worn on a tired face, was always one of absolute contentment. She radiated the deep sense of thanksgiving known only to those who realize how precious every moment of life is. I was in awe of her. Later in the day, Mary shared with the kids and staff that she had a rare and progressive condition for which there was no cure.

The ranch was humming with children, leaders, and horses working together in a concert of dust and giggles. Mary watched peacefully as her children were caught up in the happy tune. They were beautiful, quiet kids. Beyond their bright smiles and inquisitive questions lay a faint, somber maturity that young children seldom possess. It was obvious that they were fully aware of how sick their mom was, of how short their life with her might be.

Chairs were strategically placed about the ranch to ensure that Mary would always be able to sit and have a clear view of her children's progress. She and her husband moved from the hitching area to the arena, stopping from time to time to chat with the special friends who had brought them.

A high layer of clouds stretched across the sky, washing our world below in soft violet light. I was in the arena helping one of my leaders with Mary's children when I noticed that she was gone. Perhaps she needed to use the restroom, I reasoned. Not wanting her to miss any of her children's experiences, I was a little hesitant to start without her. I turned to go look for her when suddenly, to my enormous surprise, Mary herself walked in. She was wearing a helmet and leading a fully saddled horse! Kelsie, an exceptionally efficient junior leader with all the wisdom of a fourteen-year-old, was cheerfully leading Mary and the horse to the center of the arena. When they stopped, I could hear Kelsie explaining how to properly mount a horse. *She's really going to ride?* I both asked and told myself.

I felt a shiver of doubt. *Lord, is this okay?* I made my way to where Mary's husband was watching and questioned him with a look that plainly asked, "Are you sure this is all right?"

He shrugged and smiled, shaking his head. In a deep, gentle voice he simply said, "She never ceases to surprise me." His smile touched me like a warm breeze.

Immediately I sensed how important this event was. This could be Mary's defining moment. I just needed to get out of the way and let it happen. *Lord, lead the way,* I prayed silently.

They started out walking along the rail with Kelsie's tiny form marching steadily at the horse's shoulder. I could hear Mary and Kelsie talking and laughing. After several laps, Mary asked her gelding to trot. I could feel my breath catch with every rise and fall of her rusty posting within the saddle. Then—and this is something we rarely allow on a first visit—she began to canter.

Lap after lap, she flew around the arena. Friends came to the fence; cameras were brought out; even Mary's children reined in their horses and watched in amazement. We all did. Time seemed to stop. I was certain that angels were watching.

Mary's face glowed. The shadow of her illness faded beneath the radiance of those moments. The threat of death became no more than a dusty specter trampled under the horse's cantering hooves. Mary was no longer a sick woman near death. She was now just like any other mom riding with her children. In that moment she was free.

"Look at me! I'm flying! I'm flying!" she gasped, a jubilant declaration for all to hear. It felt as if she had thrown a boulder into a pond and we were all helpless to stand against the tidal wave of joy that thundered over us.

Finally, Mary slowed her horse back to a walk. I moved out to congratulate her, and then reached up and hugged her tightly in celebration. After a long moment of consideration, I told her that the horse she was riding had once nearly died. I pulled back his mane to show her the jagged ten-inch scar on his shoulder.

Mary's face grew somber. Long seconds passed. Then slowly she sat up straight and quietly pulled down the front of her pink tank top. "So did I," she said, revealing her own horrific scar—the unmistakable mark of someone who had survived having their chest split in half.

I could feel my eyes rapidly filling with tears. "Look at that," I half whispered. "The two of you are a *perfect* match."

Mary leaned over the gelding's neck and hugged him with both arms. That image of woman and horse—both survivors, both triumphant over their affliction—made a permanent imprint on my heart. What a perfect example of those who can truly wear a scar instead of allowing the scar to wear them. The blue shadows on Mary's face had vanished beneath her dazzling smile. While resting her cheek on the gelding's mane, she closed her eyes and softly said to him, "Thank you, dear one, thank you."

I pulled Kelsie into a strong hug, kissing the top of her head. Did this impish fourteen-year-old understand what she had just done—the remarkable gift that her impulsive action had given Mary? Still under my arm, Kelsie felt my gaze and looked up at my face. Her mouth spread into a wide grin. She did know—she knew *exactly!* As happens so often on the ranch, I had a fresh realization of how much I need to learn from the kids that surround me.

I dropped my gaze, shaking my head with a laugh. And then I saw them. On Kelsie's feet were the silliest pair of high-heeled white sandals that I had ever seen. Her filthy used-to-be-white socks showed through the flimsy open-toed straps.

Kelsie was in midclomp and heading out of the arena when she saw me staring at her ridiculous footwear. Looking down she quietly said, "I knew that riding without shoes was against the rules. So—" an angelic smile twinkled across her face—"I gave her mine."

hope
rising
beyond
emptiness

Black Diamond

✦

THE TINY FILLY was the runt of an already emaciated herd at the breeding ranch. Within the corral of fifteen yearlings she was jostled and bounced about like a bewildered pinball.

Hunger had forced all of the young horses to search our hands for anything that might fill their drawn bellies. But the little filly hung back, not even trying to come to us. My heart sank. Brutal experience had taught her that she would be pushed away by her taller and stronger peers.

I was struck by the way she held her head. Normally, horses in such a pitiful state will hold their heads in a neutral position to conserve what little energy they still possess. This filly held her head curiously high, not in alarm or fear, but more like…royalty. Even within starvation's grasp, she carried herself with pride and dignity—as if she held a secret, a promise known only to her. Against all odds she was managing to stay alive. And she appeared to live her life knowing something that was still yet to be.

In spite of her horribly neglected state, this filly was a shocking beauty—a deep black bay with a fine blaze and four short white socks. Her delicate face was dramatically dished in classic Arabian fashion from her enormous, heavily lashed eyes down to her teacup-sized muzzle. Her highly sculpted ears tapered into delicate tips that pointed toward each other. There was no doubt about the quality of her breeding.

She's a little black diamond, I thought. *A diamond in the rough.*

The filly took a few steps away from the herd, and my heart sank even further. Her front legs were bad, her hind legs even worse. Her pasterns, the narrow joint above the hoof, were so weak and strained that they slanted backward at an abnormal angle. A normal joint angle is approximately forty-five degrees from the ground—hers were parallel to the ground or even lower. "Oh, baby," I said under my breath as I watched her turn away.

It became clear that the owners, who were showing us around, didn't live on this property with their horses. Nor did they seem to mind their deplorable condition. Silently we moved on to the next corral, continuing our "tour." I saw little more and said even less. Outwardly I offered just enough conversation to be polite. Inwardly my heart was torn open as I cried for the hollow-eyed young horses I had just left.

Lord, show me what to do, I prayed, and I felt my heart begin to rise. Nearly all of the horses we had seen—fifty-seven to be exact—were for sale. *If this is meant to be, Lord, give us the finances to make an offer this breeder will accept.*

The vigor of summer gave way to the glory of fall. Brilliant leaves drifted to earth like a multicolored ticker-tape celebration. Then winter came to the high desert, pristine and silent, with a heavy blanket of snow.

It should have been restful, but the still-white beauty did little to soothe my aching heart. The owner had refused all our earlier offers to buy the release of any of the horses. I knew those youngsters were still out there. I knew they were still hungry.

Finally, I couldn't stand it any longer. I had to know what was happening to them. Cautiously navigating my truck through the icy conditions, I drove back down the road that led to their frozen corral. I saw that the yearlings had been moved into an open field with the adult mares. That simply meant they faced greater and stronger competition for any feed that might be provided.

But the deep snow lay undisturbed around the corral like a silent witness. There were no tracks to indicate that any feed had been delivered. There was none in the corral. The snow inside lay desolate and empty. Devoid of any human presence, the little water remaining in the trough was now frozen into a solid block.

I returned twice more in the next few days. Still there were no tracks except my own. It was clear that during this bitter season the entire herd was going without food or water. My dismay only increased when the herd began to move silently toward me in anticipation of being fed.

Then I saw her. Black Diamond, as I had begun to call the proud little filly, had deteriorated to such a degree that she had trouble negotiating the snow. Even from where I stood, I could clearly see that she was beginning to stagger.

I knew that this facility was under investigation for animal abuse. I knew the investigating officer and the attending vet. I also knew that legal wheels turn slowly. These horses needed help immediately. Not tomorrow, not next week...*today*. Now was the time for action.

I quickly came up with the idea for a pilot project for the ranch that would require many young horses. Because of the criminal investigation, I had great difficulty reaching the breeding facility by phone. But as soon as I was able, I called them to introduce the program. It would involve young horses and teenage girls. I would train the girls who would, in turn, train the horses. They would grow up together in united pairs. If both were suitable, they might later endurance race as a team.

Our ranch, I said, unfortunately lacked the financial resources to start a program of this type without some help. I carefully explained that I knew they wanted to disperse their herd. Would they be willing to sell some of their younger horses at a reduced price?

After an agonizingly slow week of negotiations, we came to a fair deal for the release of five of their young stud colts. But the black bay filly was not for sale. Under the right conditions, I was told, she would be worth nearly ten thousand dollars. For her sake alone I continued my communications with the breeding ranch.

The year moved on, and softer breezes slowly began to replace the polar bite we had grown used to in the air. My heaviest winter coat spent more time on the hook by the front door as I began to reach for a lighter one. Along with the milder weather, I received a call that warmed my heart. A youth group from near the Oregon Coast had made arrangements to spend part of their spring break to volunteer on our ranch. They wanted to offer all they had—their hands, their time, and their love.

The breeder's call came on our cell phone one cold day in early spring as Troy and I were driving home. The black bay filly was now for sale at a reasonable price. I glanced at Troy and mouthed, "Black Diamond is for sale!"

"Yes, we still want her!" I stressed. But we needed to do a thorough check of our financial resources first. Troy and I had already discussed the issue, and both of us felt strongly that we wanted to do whatever possible to help this tiny, broken filly. We also agreed that we needed to do what was financially best for the horses that we already had to support.

Troy stopped the truck as we pulled into our long drive, and I stepped out on cue to pick up our mail from the box. Back in the cab I held my hands in front of the heater vent as I flipped through the day's letters.

One small handwritten envelope caught my eye. Slicing it open with my thumb, I found inside a simple note from the youth group that was soon to arrive. "We've never done anything like this before," it began. They felt compelled, the letter said, to send us a gift. The whole group—leaders and young people—had prayed together about how much to send. Strangely enough, they had all chosen exactly the same sum.

"We're not sure what this is to be used for," the note continued. "But we *are* certain of the amount."

Enclosed with the note was a folded check, which had slipped into my lap as I read. Now I picked it up and opened it.

My jaw dropped.

It was precisely the amount needed to rescue our little black diamond.

"Okay, Lord, I believe that's clear enough," I said quietly, handing the note and check to Troy.

His eyebrows shot straight up, and laughing with me he said, "Alrighty then!"

We brought the filly home the next day.

Like a thirsty sponge, she started to fill out immediately. Her increase in weight was second only to her increase in strength. Even her weakened pasterns began to improve. Before our eyes, this little rough-cut diamond began to sparkle in the light of loving care.

Several weeks later the youth group arrived for their spring break. The sky might have been gray and gloomy, but the youth group was not. The kids tumbled out of their vans like a laughing mountain stream, thrilled to be able to stretch after their long drive. Their presence became a gift to us even before we knew their names.

After we had stowed their gear upstairs in the barn, we all met down below. I told them how grateful we were that they had offered to give up their precious free time to come and help support the ranch. The itinerary we'd mapped out for them, I continued, included helping to repair and build simple ranch structures, clearing rock, community service for a very needy ranching family, helping handicapped children to ride—and perhaps, and then I grinned, even some playtime as well!

I explained what the ranch was and what we did. I spent more time than usual emphasizing our equine rescue program. And then I began to share with that extraordinary group of kids the story of the exquisitely beautiful black bay filly. I recounted each memory I had of seeing her deteriorate before my eyes while she was imprisoned at the breeding ranch. Using my hands to explain, I told them about the condition of her weak joints—how her pasterns nearly touched the ground with each step. I went over the course of action I had taken in negotiating with the facility that owned her, and how all my efforts to move her to safety had failed.

They listened intently, their eyes growing wide and

then squeezing shut with sadness.

I explained how I felt seeing the filly on those snowy days when she was staggering with weakness and hunger. She was still not for sale.... She was far too valuable.

Without intervention, I told them, the filly was going to die.

Everywhere among the group I saw silent tears streaking down the faces of the young people. I told them how the tiny black filly finally came up for sale. How we negotiated as quickly as we could with the finances that we had.

I reminded them that when something is meant to be, it happens. "Somehow," I said, "love always seems to find a way. And today I can tell you...*your love did.*"

During my story, Troy had quietly led little Black Diamond up behind the group. Softly I said, "Would you like to meet the one your love has released?"

With open-mouthed surprise, the kids looked up as Troy led the filly in among them.

"Your love bought the release of this infant horse," I told them. "That was all she needed. Nothing more. Her life was changed forever because *your* love found a way."

The young people formed a silent circle around the filly. Every hand reached out to stroke her still-fragile body. Most young horses would have panicked at such an entrapment, but tiny Black Diamond fulfilled the promise I had seen in her that first day. She had known there was something better waiting for her, and now she basked in the rising tide of love all around her. Perhaps she somehow understood that these were the caring hands that had set her free.

Taste of Heaven

KINDNESS IS like rain in the desert. We don't ever really understand its impact until we truly know how dry the desert is. Rainlike gifts fall upon the ranch through many programs. Besides the main riding program, other offerings include a parents' support gathering, a girls' growth group, Glacier Fellowship, the Challenge team (an exercise group), a marathon running team, and Summit Seekers for hikers. Several other programs also assist in nurturing the families that come to the ranch.

Our food program is another vital asset that helps families to make ends meet. We keep a pantry and a large freezer stocked with any edible kindness that comes our way. The Village Baker, a local bakery, started the program by donating day-old bread several times a week.

Others soon followed suit by donating whatever they thought the ranch could distribute. An entire beef came, followed by hundreds of pounds of potatoes. Many donors have gone to supermarkets and brought to the ranch hundreds of dollars of items that financially-stretched families could never buy for themselves. Because it is a dynamic program, we never know when or what might be coming our way.

Such was the day when I went to simply retrieve some ice from the freezer. I opened the door—and nearly fell to my knees in astonishment! Someone had packed it full to bursting with ice cream—a frozen wall of every flavor imaginable. Sixty, eighty—maybe a hundred half-gallons.

Suddenly it became the surprise joke of the day. The leaders would instruct the kids to go and get something for them out of the freezer and then sneak around and watch their hilarious reactions. Some kids would look up in awed silence, while others would scream and laugh. A few children would even stagger backward! It was great fun.

Sierra had just arrived at the ranch—a beautiful, innocent fourteen-year-old with large, brown doelike eyes. Without preface or explanation, a small mob of younger kids pulled her by both of her arms until she stood in front of the freezer.

I came around the corner just in time to see her reaction, which occurred in slow motion. Her already large eyes dilated into huge black pearls. Her jaw dropped until it was not humanly possible for her mouth to open any larger. She staggered a step backward as her lips formed the syllable "Oh." Time stopped as her brain tried to comprehend the sheer grandeur of the frozen wall of ice cream that rose before her.

Still gazing upward and distracted by nothing, in a hallowed, blissful voice she finally whispered, "It's heaven…within heaven."

The Glass Pony

❦

I WAS ONLY seven. Sleeping over at Grandma Mimi's house was one of the highlights of my life.

Playing in the orchard behind her house, snuggling with her on the couch, and eating enormous amounts of fresh-baked goodies made my life with grandma a little slice of heaven. Her love transformed her simple country home into a child's paradise.

Toward the end of a visit, I often would hide myself in the bushes from my patient mother with the hope that she would "forget" me there, allowing me to spend the night with Mimi. While peeking through peony leaves, I would watch the dust slowly roil up from behind my mother's car as she made her way back up the dirt driveway. When my grandmother tucked me into bed in one of my grandpa's T-shirts, it made me feel like the most special girl on earth.

Just outside my window at my grandparents' house stood an enormous oak tree. At night I could see tiny, distant stars winking down at me through the looming, black branches. And at times the moon smiled into the room with a pearly glow.

There, on the windowsill itself, the soft light danced off the back of a small glass pony. From my bed I could only make out the soft reflection of its face, neck, and back. It was gray in any light, its little face cast into a permanent smile that pressed against its large round cheeks. But when moonlight flooded over that glass pony and all of the world that I could see, it beckoned me to wonder and to dream. *Would I ever have my own horse?*

For many young girls, having a horse of their own ranks high on the scale of importance, right up there with breathing.

I would lie in bed, drifting in and out of slumber's grasp, dreaming of sharing my life with *my* horse. In sleep's drifting images I galloped over clover fields and swam in every pond. I lived with my face buried in tousled mane and earthy scent. My horse and I galloped, screaming for the joy of life, laughing with arms outstretched over fields and streams. We soared together flying on the wings of the wind.

Lying there in the dark, I could feel my horse's velvet muzzle next to my face. Such are the blissful dreams of a seven-year-old's heart.

Troy and I were enjoying a break on the beautiful Oregon coast.

When we have a rare spare moment, my husband loves to indulge me in one of my favorite pastimes. Fortified with gigantic cups of flavored coffee, we stroll arm in arm in mindless decadent leisure, cruising the antique stores. I love to ponder the stories these items could tell.

I always justify these times by telling myself that I am looking for fun Western items—tidbits to make the ranch more appealing and whimsical for the kids. Although nearly everything is out of my price range, the looking is still free. With the twinkling eye of a treasure hunter, I begin each foray with the conviction in my simple heart that today—maybe—I will find something spectacular.

I hummed softly to myself and allowed my eyes to aimlessly explore the vast array of offerings as Troy and I drifted from aisle to aisle. My heart roamed free; it was like being pushed aimlessly by an afternoon breeze as we drifted along in relaxed bliss.

Then we rounded the end of an aisle...and I saw it. A soft "ohh" poured from my lips. A flood of memories washed over my heart as I reached out to pick it up. Its cool, smooth surface was as familiar to me as it had been when I was seven. This one was tan instead of gray, but otherwise it was exactly the same. It was the glass pony that had lived on the windowsill of my grandparents' home when I was a child. The pony that had inspired my dreams and watched over me at night.

Quietly I explained to Troy how I remembered the glass pony. At seven, it had been my dreamland playmate when I visited Grandma Mimi and was always waiting for me on the bedroom windowsill. After the deaths of my parents, when I was nine, I moved into that same bedroom...permanently.

It was during these times that I began to imagine the glass pony not as my dreamy playmate but as my guardian. I hoped that it would protect me from the new terrors of the night. Only then could I slip into a dreamless refuge from the pain of my loss.

Somehow that glass pony was transformed into a figurehead—representing protection in my dreams from childhood, and now, representing a life fulfilled. Seeing it again had abruptly swung my heart into a full circle.

I was still wandering in my ineffective explanation as Troy silently lifted the glass pony out of my hands. He wore a soft, all-knowing smile that communicated without words his understanding. Arm in arm, he guided me to the front of the store toward the cashier, where he bought the glass pony for me.

I sat with my grandma in front of the big western-facing window in her home, taking in the incredible view of the Cascade Mountains. The sunshine poured in all around us like a brilliant golden blanket. Monday was our day together. Our special time. We ate dinner together and talked about all that has happened between us since our last visit. With detailed descriptions, I shared the highlights of what Troy and I saw and did on our brief trip. I also used dramatic hand gestures because my grandma, a tiny soul near ninety, was almost completely blind.

She still chose to live in her own house, alone. Her rising determination and strength always amazed me. We reminisced of times past and speculated of times to come. We talked about everything. Between us, those were precious moments.

I began to tell my grandma about our trip through the antique store. I told her in great detail how I had found the glass pony and the flood of emotion that came with it. "Grandma," I asked, "do you remember the gray pony that used to be in the windowsill of my bedroom? It was in our home when we all lived down by Shasta Lake."

She turned momentarily and looked out of the window. It seemed as though she were trying to remember. I tried to fill the gaps in her memory that time had erased.

She turned back toward me. Her chin rested on her thumb while her index finger crossed her lips. She began to nod slightly in vague recollection. I could only imagine how difficult it was for her to try to mentally locate a glass item in a home that she hadn't seen in twenty years. Wincing to myself, I thought, *I can't even remember what I had for lunch yesterday!*

I told her that I hadn't seen the glass pony since she and Grandpa had moved to Bend twenty years ago. I guessed that it had been sold in their moving sale before they left Redding.

With her chin still resting on her thumb and her eyebrows drawn tightly together, she simply said, "Perhaps."

Grandma left the room for a moment, and I mentally kicked myself for not remembering to bring the tan version of the glass pony. She would have enjoyed that so much.

My thoughts shifted gears again. *How could I have ever let something so important to me just slip away?* I wondered. I guess that I really didn't understand how important it was until I saw its tan copy. In all of my fumbling explanation to Troy, I realized now how symbolic the glass pony was and that in reality, it was my...

"Honey! Look!"

Startled, my head snapped around to see my little grandma stepping down into the living room. "Do you mean *this* pony?" she beamed as she held it out to me.

"Oh, Grandma...."

The tears of a little girl began to fill my eyes as I gently lifted it from her. Its gray color and smooth roundish surface were exactly how I remembered. "Yes, Grandma, this is it," I quietly said through falling tears.

"Honey, it's yours. It's always been yours," she said, as she placed her hand on my arm. The image of this small, laughing pony embodied the journey of my life.

Holding it in my hands was like holding the very figurehead of my own heart. As a child, I could have never known the incredible significance of this small glass horse. As an adult, looking back, its powerful symbolism astounded me.

Finally, through the rushing swirl of emotions, my thoughts cleared enough to say, "Grandma, I don't think that I realized until just now...this was my very first horse."

My precious little grandma, the one who by God's strength saved my life, fell gravely ill. While surrounded by those who loved her, only weeks before the completion of this book, she let go of this life with her left hand and with her right received the outstretched hand of her Heavenly Father. In a single moment I lost my grandmother, my mother, and my best friend. But the truth is she is not lost at all. I will see her again, and until then, I will lay hold of the strength, love, and hope she infused into my life.

In Cherished Memory
Beth Everest
May 25, 1913–August 1, 2002

Victor's Boy

THROUGHOUT THE season the ranch hosts dozens of groups that come to visit, ride, or volunteer. Each group brings with it a special "flavor" that all combine to add richness to what the ranch is becoming. The Haven Project, a nonprofit organization that pairs inner-city children with professional actors, is one of our favorite groups. Together, actor and child rehearse for a local production while being sheltered under the protective wings of friendship and trust.

The Haven kids are especially funny, happy, and playful. They truly bring out the best in me, my staff, and apparently everyone that their smiles spread over. We always look forward to our time with them.

Victor is one of the adult actors who volunteers for The Haven Project. His large, commanding James Earl Jones presence is completely balanced by his soft-spoken kindness.

The children streamed out of the school bus like a multicolored ribbon, and I looked for Victor. In moments, however, the happy chaos consumed my attention.

Seven horses had been brought out, and all of the kids had been divided into alternating grooming and riding teams. The squealing excitement settled into a busy hum, and I turned to see Victor approaching with his wife and their two beautiful little girls.

"Victor!" I cheered, and I threw my arms around his neck in a welcome hug. Even through his completely gentle response, I could detect that he was distracted.

I noticed that as we quietly conversed, he was politely looking over and around me. Subconsciously, I turned slightly to try and see the object of his search. With a fraction of anxiety he asked, "Is he still here? Is my big boy still here?"

Immediately I realized that he was looking for Luke, the giant draft horse that Victor fell in love with the previous year.

"Yes, Luke is right over there," I said, pointing into the main corral. "I was waiting for the hitching area to clear out a little so that I could bring him out for you."

I could tell that Victor didn't really hear me. He quickly moved away as if being pulled by a magnificent golden magnet. Luke, as if on cue, moved to the rail and reached over to greet Victor.

Over the mild chaos I watched them. With the tender touch of a father, Victor cradled the massive draft horse's head in his big hands. I could see that he was speaking softly to Luke. A big man gently getting reacquainted with his big horse.

It was a wonderfully sincere moment that I felt privileged to witness.

I continued to watch as Troy waded through the kids and hailed a greeting to Victor. The big man turned toward my husband. The warmth from his expression was radiant; I could literally *feel* it from where I stood. He was beaming as he looked at Troy and quietly said, "You don't know how much I have looked forward to this moment. I rode this horse last year. In my heart...I have ridden him every day since."

Simple Gifts

EIGHT INCHES of perfect white blanketed Central Oregon, muting every sound into a hushed lullaby. It was an unusually heavy snowfall for November. For Cheree, a single mother, it marked the first year that she had carved out a simple life in the country with her daughter. A year since they had moved from their small rental in town to a house of their own on a handful of acres—a fixer-upper that, side by side, they were working to make into their dream home. A year during which they had strategically planned and saved so they could realize their vision for a new life together.

Thanksgiving came and along with it the usual multitude of pre-Christmas sales. Because it was the only time they could afford to do so, Cheree and her daughter weathered the crowds and traffic to complete all of their Christmas shopping.

Beneath their snow-covered roof, they found great comfort in their simple home with a few simple gifts. With their shopping behind them, mother and daughter settled into the season, putting up their meager Christmas decorations with a deep sense of satisfaction.

The holiday season's mail brought its usual mixture of blessings and bills. After work one day, Cheree sat down to thumb through the daily stack. She came to a familiar envelope that enclosed the support check used to help cover their house payment and provide for her daughter. It always came with reassuring predictability, and her mind was already on other things as she sliced open the envelope and removed the check. Her tired eyes fell on it only briefly...but then zeroed in on the little figures. Her mind snapped into sharp focus. Her chin dropped. Her hand holding the check began to tremble.

It was made out for less than one-eighth of the normal amount.

Disaster! Without that money she wouldn't be able to cover their house payment. In a single instant, the blessing Cheree had felt in being able to buy and give gifts during this Christmas season had turned into a crushing burden. Cheree's heart hammered painfully as she allowed her gaze to wander around the warm kitchen that she and her daughter had worked so hard to turn into the welcoming center of their new home. Her mind twisted around a single thought: What were they going to do?

"Please don't tell *anyone* where these came from." A true philanthropist, my friend pressed into my hands nearly a dozen generous gift certificates from a local clothing store. "I'm trusting you to see they're given to the people who need them most."

Lord, show me where these belong, I prayed as I drove from work back to the ranch.

The following afternoon we had our girls' group meeting in our house. The gathering provides a safe environment for girls to share their challenges and victories with leaders and peers in small groups. After the girls prayed for each other, everyone came together for a time of simple instruction on teen issues.

Meanwhile, the mothers met in a separate room, where they supported each other in much the same way. Half of the women were single mothers struggling to raise their children with little or no help at all. Encouragement and support of any kind were always appreciated by these weary souls.

I crept unannounced into their group, the bearer of anonymous good news. With quiet stealth I passed out the certificates, briefly sharing with each mother how I had come by these gifts. All were grateful. But when I placed two certificates into Cheree's hands, she gripped them with white-knuckled fists as though they were a steering wheel. She closed her eyes, and tears streaked down her cheeks.

The room fell silent.

Finally, when she was able, Cheree spoke softly. "You can't know what this means." She gave a ragged sigh before she explained how this was going to be their first real Christmas. She told us about the excitement she and her daughter had shared, about carefully budgeting and buying all their gifts during the Thanksgiving sales. And then the disaster of the minimized support check.

"After a lot of prayer and consideration, we both agreed that there was only one option," Cheree said, looking down at the floor. "A home is a home. We have nothing without it. We decided together that we needed to do whatever it took to make the house payment. It was hard...."

She wiped her face and looked up in exhausted triumph. "So we took them all back. Every single gift we'd bought. And with a few other changes, we were able to make our house payment."

Cheree let her breath out slowly. "We agreed that this year our gift would be our home. It was the right decision, and it was enough," she added, with a decisive little dip of her chin.

She looked down again at the gift certificates clutched in her hands. "I never expected this." Her voice trailed off and she murmured, "God is so faithful."

The moment washed over everyone in a tearful wave of encouraging hugs and laughter. "I think," Cheree said thoughtfully, wiping her face, "that I'll use this to buy my daughter a letterman jacket. She deserves it. Last year she lettered in academics with a 4.0. I was never able to afford a jacket...until now."

She looked at the understanding faces around the room. "We'd accepted what we had to go without. But instead, this has turned out to be the *best* Christmas ever."

My heart traveled from the warm glow of that moment to the generous person who had made it possible. I hoped that the joy the gift had produced would take wing and find him. I hoped he would know his part in proving God's faithfulness, because he had followed in the tradition of the greatest Giver of gifts—the One who makes every Christmas the best ever.

hope
rising
across all
seasons

The Patriot

*A*MID OUR DOZEN horses a small army of excited children stampeded about, arms loaded with decorations in preparation for the parade. The familiar marble rattle of spray paint cans being shaken made the very air sound happy. My patient horses yielded their bodies as living canvases for the young artists eager to paint their soft glowing hides with glittering stars and stripes. Red, white, and blue decorations were strewn in every direction beneath the bright morning sun. Here, within the hub of joyful chaos, my heart soared. It was the best of days—it was the Fourth of July.

I looked at my paint-drenched horses, standing innocent as lambs. *God bless them,* crossed my mind, quickly followed by the thought, *He already has.* My heart smiled.

It was almost time. After all of the fluffing, combing, glittering, and painting, the kids and horses were nearly ready. I surveyed the aftermath of the happy onslaught. The sparkling debris on the ground made the earth itself shine with a dazzling grin.

Now we were ready. And I was prepared to share with our star-spangled herd what this day was really all about. I gathered everyone together—children in front, adults at the back—and began to share my heart, my simple view of what this day represented. I wanted the kids to understand that this parade was not for them; it was not about them. It was to honor the brave souls in uniform whose unfaltering service to our great land ensured our freedom. Only a few of those soldiers had survived to see this day; fewer still were able to celebrate with us in the parade. Today was *their* day. They had fought to win the liberty and independence we now enjoyed under peaceful skies.

I looked down into their open and winsome faces. The kids were hearing every word. They were feeling how important this was. Through my own ineptitude, I tried to explain how much these brave men and women gave to protect their country, their homes, their families...and us. They did their job out of their sense of honor, and in return to them we showed them our honor out of respect and gratitude.

I could feel my throat drawing tight and tears starting to rise. A mother in the back, openly moved, wiped her eyes. Seeing her compassion, my fragile dam gave way. I dropped my head, and I wept.

Quiet moments passed. Music and the clattering of hooves and creaking of wagons—sounds of the assembling parade—floated our way. It was nearly time to go. But there was one more thing that needed to be said.

In a soft voice I implored the children to think about something that evening while watching the fireworks with their families. "When you look into the deep night sky, you know that every light, every single spark that ignites the darkness, burns hot and then burns out. Remember that each one represents a life that was given. A life that burned bright and then burned out...so that you and I could be free. Freedom is not free. It has been earned for us by thousands who gave their all, who gave everything, who gave their lives, so that you and I could share in their victory. So that we could share in the freedom that they gave their lives to protect. Our job today is to seek out the veterans who are here and thank them."

The reminder was in place. Now we were ready.

With full hearts we marched on to the parade route. Each horse could have been flown from a flagpole—so dazzling were their proud decorations. Jubilant, waving children sat astride their bannered backs, shining in head-to-toe patriotism. I walked out leading my horse and her young rider into the last position.

We squeezed down the street between waving flags and ruby-cheeked faces, and I looked for an opportunity to express my thanks personally to some of the veterans. Halfway through the parade, between the freckled faces and sticky-fingered waves, I saw him.

He sat in a wheelchair much too large for his frail body. His hands, crippled with age, were folded on his blanketed lap. His body was ravaged by time, but he proudly wore on his sagging white head a neatly creased olive drab cap with the unmistakable insignia of a World War II veteran.

Within the shrunken shell of his body there still lived the indomitable spirit of a man who was proud to have served his country. And now, in the twilight of his years, he wanted people to remember him...to remember that he was a veteran. I was captured by him.

I could only imagine the man that he once had been. Young and powerful, with an honest heart that sought not only to serve himself, but also the greater good of our nation's integrity. That young man was still there, his spirit still glowing deep within the old man's eyes.

With horse and child in tow I paused, trying to gain the

old soldier's attention. I tipped my cowboy hat to him and said a loud, "Thank you!" His rheumy eyes came into focus, and his head snapped up. His lips parted as he stared at me. His expression seemed to say, *Are you talking to me?*

The parade moved me along, but I twisted around to keep him in sight, hoping he understood me, hoping he knew that I was thanking him. It was far too important a moment to let it slip by.

His eyebrows furrowed together as he tried to read the emotions on my face. He didn't seem to realize that I was talking just to him, so I made it easy for him. I removed my hat and pressed it to my chest in an expression of honor and looked directly into his eyes—behind his eyes to where the young soldier still lived. And I said, "What you have done has not been forgotten."

For a second his face contorted with the pain of long-suppressed memories. And then a torrent of tears flooded his weathered cheeks. He caught them all, dropping his face into his cupped hands. His shoulders crumpled forward. One sob after another shook his frail body in an effort to be free. I watched him over my shoulder until a shifting crowd of devoted young well-wishers enveloped him.

Wow, Lord! What just happened? I pondered the question as I moved on down the parade route. My intent had been to honor the veteran, not to crush him beneath a wave of grief. My heart was devastated. Had I inadvertently ripped open an ancient scar? Had my blundering expression of respect pushed him back into a theater that, for decades, he had been trying to forget? Or had his thoughts flashed back to a foreign battlefield where, once again, he watched as his brothers' lives, like the fireworks, had flamed with staggering passion, burned bright, and then were burned out before him.

This veteran, who had been sitting so peacefully watching the parade until I spoke to him, was seemingly ambushed by my clumsy attempt at appreciation. Where did his thoughts go? What did he see in his mind's eye to prompt such a visceral response? My naive heart could never visualize, much less comprehend, the images that must have flooded his soul.

Even though I continued to wave and smile at the crowds, cool bewilderment crept over my heart. *Lord, instead of healing...did I hurt?* For the rest of the parade, I was left to wonder.

The parade drew to a close, and our entourage returned to its staging area, where everyone was abuzz about their many adventures during the trip down Main Street. I heard numerous stories of how several of those in uniform received all the love, honor, and respect our little team knew how to give. I was so proud of them all. Clearly they had understood the message I'd tried to communicate to them before the parade. And with childlike innocence they had carried it out. They had given honor where it was due. They had shown respect to those who had earned it long ago.

It had been a stellar day. All but for the uncertainty still troubling me over my encounter with the veteran in the wheelchair. My thoughts were interrupted. "Kim!" One of the parents, a friend of mine, called to me. He waved me over and told me he had been standing near the veteran and had watched as the old soldier wept long after the parade had swept us out of his sight.

My imagination began recreating the scene as my friend relayed a detailed description of all that he had observed. The elderly man continued to quietly weep, evidently consumed by his private grief.

Then, after his silent storm passed, he drew out a worn handkerchief, used it to dry his face, and carefully returned it to his pocket. It was as if that action had wiped the pain away with his tears, and then his transformation began. The frail old man, slumped in his wheelchair without the strength to hold his head higher than his chest, had been washed away in his flood of tears. The new man, still elderly and wheelchair bound, with a great effort moved his shoulders back until they rested firmly against his chair. In a motion that was most certainly painful, he moved his once-hanging head back and up until he held it at military attention between his newly squared shoulders.

My friend's description of what he had seen reflected my exact thoughts: True patriotism is not confined or diminished by age.

I'll never know what transpired in the patriot's heart that day. Perhaps he returned to a time when the winds of war blew. In a mighty struggle known only to God, he was able to bend as the storms swept over him. By God's mercy, as the smoke lifted, he was still left standing. Although today the tempest raged with fierce savagery, it blew itself out of the present and into the past. The boy who survived was transformed into a victorious man. Even now, within his failing body, he remained the victor.

Within my heart is a vault of heroes. Some are as close as my own soul; some I have never met. When I think of him now, the patriot, I will always remember him as one of their treasured number—someone who inspires me to become a better person. I will always remember him as my hero.

Tanked

⟨ornament⟩

BIRTHDAYS ARE always special events on the ranch. When one of our kids, young or old, declares, "Today is my birthday," they set into motion a stealthy chain of events that can't be stopped. We don't spank or pinch or sing traditional songs. But an observant soul might witness a knowing eyebrow being raised between each of our leaders.

Cake and ice cream are always welcome, but they never distract us from our focus. Our habitually kind and gentle staff, grinning like Cheshire cats, are silently transformed into single-minded hunters. Once the "birthday bait" has been captured, no amount of begging, bargaining, or pleading will save their one-year-older soul.

We drag or carry them, hand and foot, kicking and squealing, to their fate. Wriggling and laughter quickly turn into wide-eyed mock horror as we carry our captive through the main corral gate. Even the horses seem to enjoy the sacrificial rite, gathering around as we begin swinging our hapless victims to the count of three. With a mighty toss we let them fly into the face of a day they won't soon forget. "Happy Birthdays" rain down in a torrential shower as they land with a flailing, spread-eagled splash in the horses' water tank.

Solemn Vow

THE BITTER December wind nipped at my cheeks and ears as I stepped out of my dependable, old Dodge truck. The sky hung above like a thick, gray quilt. There would be snow before dusk, falling like glitter flung from the hand of God.

I had made the long drive out to this rundown ranch a number of times, drawn by my concern over the herd of starving horses. This time I was meeting with the owner. I walked across the frozen ground to where she waited and gave her a hug as I recalled earlier conversations with her. I had the strong impression that this woman, like her horses, had known great personal suffering. Despite my anguish over the condition of her horses, I still understood that she needed to be treated with compassion and respect.

Together we approached the herd, and I sucked in my breath at the sight of a young black mare. Her condition was hideous. Even through her heavy black winter coat I could see that she was severely emaciated—far more than the others. But something about her called out to me.

Her gaunt frame was so underdeveloped that my closed fist could not fit between her front legs. Adding substantially to her plight was the fact that she was the herd outcast. Rejected by her own kind, she was driven away from what little food existed to forage in the brambles alone.

She was like every other child I've ever known, starving for all of the physical and emotional sustenance that gives hope to live another day. And like too many children, she knew none of these things. Time for her was running out. Like a battered child, she wouldn't raise her head or even lift her eyes to look at me. My presence seemed to inspire only more fear in a heart that had already been tattered by more sorrow than she could bear. Like a shadow cast by nothing she silently skirted away.

She reminded me of many of the children I work with—conditioned by long periods of rejection, they learn to fall back into the shadows, to say nothing, to think nothing, to be nothing. In full view of the world they gradually wither and disappear. We've all seen them. The children who hang back in a group. The children who prefer the lonely, protective shelter of a corner over the pain of more rejection and embarrassment. The ones who become the whipping post for every bully. They are like woolly sweaters matted with every imaginable mean-spirited burr. They are the soft, innocent heads that are chosen last for every game.

For so many of these precious lambs, going home at the end of the day does not bring relief. There is no comfort. There is no safety. Only more abuse and terror. For some, going home is like an innocent lamb going to slaughter.

Blinking hard, I looked back up at the devastated filly. Her dusty hide bore the wounds of her rejection. She was the equine version of the sacrificial lamb. In her herd— what should have been her family—she was the unclaimed soul, the silent, hungry breeze, the shadowy pariah with nowhere to turn for comfort.

I turned to the owner. *Go carefully, Kim,* I warned myself. I masked my sense of urgency with a nonchalant tone. "How much for that young black mare?"

"Her?" The owner's tone of voice indicated that had the horse been for sale her selling price had just gone up. But any hopes I had of rescuing the horse were crushed when the owner said, "She's not for sale. She's being kept for a breeding program, to produce highly valued black and white foals."

I kept my expression neutral, but inwardly felt a stab of pain. The mare was not even three years old—far too young to carry a foal even if she had been in perfect condition. But she was not. Her twisted forelegs were barely able to support her wasted frame. This phantom of a filly was missing at least a third of her normal body weight, and she was receiving too little food even to maintain that—let alone to sustain a foal. Conception for her would be impossible...or fatal.

I revealed nothing of the turmoil I felt inside. I said nothing. We talked on about many other horses, many other things. But deep inside my thoughts were focused on the mare. I ran through one scenario after another, trying to figure out a way to negotiate her release. Within my heart I prayed, *Lord, please show me the way. Please show me how to help this solemn little one.*

The call finally came. It had been six months since I had last seen the black filly. Her hollow, downcast gaze had continued to haunt my heart. Now, still swaying on crooked legs, she was for sale. Negotiations for her purchase were completed by the end of my conversation with the owner.

Sarah, one of my senior staff, came with me two weeks later on the four-hour journey to pick up the horse and bring her home. We chatted excitedly all the way. The release of "Solemn," as we had christened her, was such a huge answer to prayer that we knew it was right and that everything was going to be okay.

At last we pulled into the driveway and maneuvered cautiously between the rusty old cars, piles of rotting wood, and discarded appliances, looking for a safe place to position the horse trailer. We expected that this would be Solemn's first experience being loaded into a trailer, and we wanted to minimize her terror as much as possible. Once we had parked, Sarah and I warmly greeted the owner. Together we skirted the multitude of chained-up dogs, blocking our ears to their frenzied barking. Finally we came to the dilapidated corral where the filly had been left tied up.

With each advancing step my throat closed a little more. Perhaps time had gentled the memory I had of her, but without the camouflage of her winter coat her condition was shocking. Her ridged spine towered over a ribcage so jagged that it resembled a dinosaur display. Her breastbone jutted forward like the bow of a ship, three inches out from the surrounding flesh. Her bony hips protruded so savagely that it seemed they might slice through the fragile hide straining to cover them. Her legs, back, face, and rump were zigzagged with jagged cuts and scratches—all about two weeks old. The wounds on her face were bad, but the gash on her leg was worse. It should have been stitched when it happened. Now it was too late. It gaped open, caked with dried blood and manure. More than likely, infection had already set in.

My heart pounded and my neck and scalp prickled as

raw emotion coursed through me. The owner chattered on pleasantly as we made our way to the corral. Stealthily I glanced at Sarah. Her eyes shimmered with suppressed anger and sorrow. Her beautiful lips were pulled into a hard, flat line. I knew that she would not trust herself to speak until we were safely back in the privacy of the truck.

Solemn literally shook at our approach. She had pushed her head into the corner behind the post where she was tied in a futile effort to hide herself from us. Her haunches quivered like aspen leaves in the wind. I wanted to cry. I wanted to scream. I wanted to cradle her head against my chest and promise this broken creature that she would never be hurt again.

But I couldn't do any of those things. Instead, we silently watched a pitiful demonstration of what this terrified horse could do. She was shuddering under the weight of a heavy western saddle. In her mouth was a gag bit made of twisted iron, which was certainly adding to the pain of her deplorable physical condition. She recoiled violently from every touch as though she were being shocked. The glaring whites of her dilated eyes silently screamed of her life of horror.

Finally I couldn't bear it any more. Guarding myself to keep an even tone, I asked the owner to please remove the saddle and bridle. We signed a makeshift bill of sale, and I paid what I owed, praying all the while that Solemn would allow herself to be loaded into our trailer without further injury.

With gentle encouragement, Sarah and I were able to lead our new charge toward the open trailer. But faced with the open door she spread her crooked front legs out like a young giraffe bowing for a drink. Her eyes bulged with terror as she began to snort and blow.

A frightened horse will sometimes struggle so violently during an attempt to load it into a trailer that it wounds itself to the point of self-destruction. *Dear Lord,* I silently prayed, *please don't let that happen to Solemn.*

We let her stand quietly, giving her time to explore and accept this strange claustrophobic block in front of her. Then the owner casually walked past her and up into the open trailer with an armload of hay. I bit back my experienced opinion that hunger never triumphs over blinding, life-threatening fear. That arrogant thought was scarcely formed in my mind before the filly's eyes focused on that life-giving nourishment, and her feral instinct took over. She lurched toward the food, not even seeming to notice the step up into the trailer in her famished effort to get as much hay as she could before, once again, she was driven away. With sad amazement I quietly closed the trailer door behind her.

I peered at her through the drop window in the side of the trailer. Her enormous eyes were still rimmed with fear, but she chewed steadily at the hay.

We said our good-byes quickly and wove our way out of the yard and onto the highway, driving as though we were hauling a glass horse. She very nearly was. In her condition any sudden movement could jostle her into a broken pile on the trailer floor.

Sarah, having restrained her volcanic anger all this time, erupted in fury the moment we were out of earshot. We both have seen this kind of thing many times, but it is something we will never get used to. Gradually, as the miles went by and we drew closer to home, we both relaxed. Sarah and I returned to the normal rhythm of our conversations and mapped out our strategy of how we were going to help Solemn.

Once we had her safely back at the ranch, there was much to do. She was vaccinated and dewormed and then settled into the quarantine paddock. We took her height and weight as a baseline measurement for progress. Even though we moved around her as calmly as we could, she still trembled and jerked pathetically, like a tattered flag snapping in the wind. We tended to all her wounds, including the oozing gash on her leg. She let us do anything as long as we didn't move her away from her food.

The next day her condition had visibly improved. On her grotesquely shrunken frame, simple hydration made a clear difference.

Solemn's progress spiked initially, but after several months it seemed to level out. As she became stronger physically, we noticed an emotional change. Instead of cowering when someone approached her, she was now strong enough to wheel and run. Her body was growing, but her faith in humans was not. Life for her—as for so many abused children—had been far too cruel for far too long. *How deeply,* I wondered, *can trust be beaten down before it can no longer be resurrected?*

Day after day I entered her corral, hoping to build a bridge of trust. Sadly, I watched as she instead began her familiar pattern of evasive maneuvers. Between us a new foundation needed to be built. "Think of me as the gentle boss mare," I told her. "I'll never hurt you. You are my herd. I will love you with my life. All I'm asking is for you to trust me enough to turn and face me."

It was disheartening, after so many months, that she was still too terrified even to look at me, let alone turn toward me. Every session ended the same way. Quietly I would approach her flank and gently stroke her hips and back. Inch by inch my slowly circling hands would move up to her shoulder. It was in this position that I spent the most time, stroking as much of her quivering black hide as I could reach. She nearly always stood with her head lowered, deeply pressed into a corner of the fence or some other hiding place. I hated seeing this awesome, powerful creature cowering at my touch.

Then without warning a significant change occurred. A tiny crack broke through the thick wall of fear that guarded Solemn's heart. Suddenly, instead of seeking escape, she stopped, lowered her head, and looked at me. Hearing my startled intake of breath, she turned to face me! Everything seemed to stop, including my heart. I held my breath, fearing that any movement would frighten her away. Her eyes were wide and questioning. Her head bobbed and dipped, wavering between the high, alarmed position that precedes sudden flight, and a low, submissive posture that pleaded for acceptance.

Slowly I turned away, inviting her to follow. Time slipped away between us. Then in carefully measured movements, I backed toward her. Her head and neck arched backward, but her hooves stayed firmly planted.

I paused. Her neck began to relax, and she stretched her head out toward me. With all the speed of a rising moon, I held one finger in front of her velvet muzzle. I peered cautiously over my shoulder, and I watched as her nostrils flared slightly to take in my scent. The investigation seemed to satisfy her; she did not retreat. Now she stood only inches from me.

With the tenderness of an angel's kiss, I crooked my

index finger and touched the space between her nostrils.
It was as soft as a butterfly's wing. It was the first time that
she came to me actually searching for the comfort of my
hand. That moment flooded my heart with warmth. From
then on, each day built upon the last. She allowed me to
touch her muzzle, her cheek, her forehead—and finally
her neck and body. Working with her was like stringing a
precious necklace one pearl at a time. Each improvement,
no matter how small, brought with it a cascade of praise.
Each baby step on its own seemed unimpressive. But I
knew that the sum of them all could take us to the top of
the highest mountain.

Kids and staff had started working with her also. She
was regularly brushed, combed, clipped, and bathed. She
flourished under their care like a rose in the early summer
sun. Her physical condition improved in tandem with the
emotional change. Within weeks she had added a hundred
and thirty pounds to her once-skeletal frame. Now faint
dapples began to appear on her shining coat.

Even so, her trickle of confidence had grown into only
a modest stream. The dam of fear that shielded her heart
was still firmly in place, blocking her from any open
demonstration of love. She was still deeply distrustful of
humans. I wondered if she would make it. Could she
become a usable horse for adults? Could she ever cross
that rare threshold to become a great children's horse?

Sondra sat alone in the rumbling isolation of the airline
cabin. Fifteen thousand feet above the Cascade
Mountains, she was lost in a mountain range of thoughts
as vast as the peaks far below.

She and her three teenage children had survived a difficult divorce. Now, having hopscotched from city to city across the United States, she was desperately determined to find the right place where she could safely nurture and raise her family.

Her oldest and youngest children were bright and academically gifted. They were resilient, like daisies, thriving wherever they were planted. But her middle daughter, Emily, was struggling to find where she fit in her new world.

Emily had the soul of an artist. Her feelings, like tender young shoots, were easily bruised and damaged by the thoughtless trampling of her peers. She was a fragile budding rose. And every day all the substance and softness that was Emily was quietly, petal by petal, falling away. She needed something, or someone, special, something uniquely hers to pour her emotions into. And she needed it soon.

Gazing down at the snow-capped peaks, Sondra felt the first stirring of hope. The mountains beckoned her like long-lost friends. They whispered comfort to her bruised heart. They became part of her answer. In spite of the shoulder-to-shoulder confinement of the stuffy airplane, her spirit began to soar. It rose up before God like a weary sparrow, searching for shelter in the relentless storm of her life.

Where there is safety, there is rest. With rest comes clarity of thought. Above the whispering mountains, Sondra's immediate future crystallized, and she made her decision. The community nestled in the hills far below would become her family's new home. Finally the weary bird came safely to rest, nestled deep within the presence of God.

Sondra called me after making the decision to move to Central Oregon. Her love for her children clearly came across the telephone line. She showed special concern for Emily, her talented middle child, who seemed to be having the most trouble adjusting to their new life. I encouraged her to bring her two girls to the ranch the following Saturday.

The ranch was at rest under a cool, bright afternoon sky when their car wound its way up the hill and stopped in the main yard. What I noticed first about Sondra were her dark, intelligent eyes, whimsically framed by round glasses. Her easy laugh hinted at a household that was often filled with girlish giggles and fun. Yet the intensity in her gaze revealed her inner strength—and the ferocity of a lioness ready to protect her cubs. I liked her immediately.

She introduced me to her two daughters. Emily and Lauren were fourteen and sixteen, both with the innocent, impish beauty of girls who honestly don't know how lovely they are. They were warm and only a little shy. I took them around our small ranch on a detailed tour until there was only one paddock left to visit. I was following my hunch.

"These are all youngsters we've rescued this year," I told the girls, naming the horses and sharing the stories of how they came to be at the ranch. Three inquisitive little geldings reached over and through the fence poles, happily seeking any hand that might offer a snack or a good scratch.

The sisters giggled a bit as they reached from muzzle to muzzle to greet the curious colts. I have seen the delighted expressions on the faces of thousands of youngsters, but I never cease to be moved by them. The girls' attention was lost to everything but the eagerly questing creatures before them. With mouths slightly open, lifted in silent smiles, the sisters were filled with wonder, their eyes twinkling with possibilities and love. They were utterly captured in the moment.

Then to my great surprise, Solemn approached us as softly as a breeze. From the back of the small herd, her unmistakable black muzzle reached toward Emily's outstretched fingers.

Contact—with a total stranger.

Despite my amazement I wondered if on an emotional level the girl and the filly were strangers after all. Emily turned to me with a radiant smile. "What's this one's name?" she asked, stroking the filly's cheek.

"Solemn," I told her, watching this remarkable breakthrough with fascination. The girl, of course, was oblivious to the magnitude of what was happening. "Emily," I said. "I have an idea...."

Within minutes we had groomed Solemn. A beaming Emily led her into the round pen. Together, she and I would work with the horse from the ground. I gave Emily a quick briefing on how horses communicate and the kind of response we hoped Solemn would give. I encouraged Emily to relax and to move easily around the center of the pen so that I could puppet her movements from behind.

Solemn began to trot around us, and I whispered steadily into Emily's ear, explaining what the filly was doing—alternately looking for escape or for acceptance. I also told her how the horse might interpret what we were doing.

The horse glided around us, black, long-legged, cantering with fluid grace. I crouched awkwardly behind Emily as we tried to coordinate our movements. I told her that what we were doing might not work. So far a breakthrough was beyond Solemn's ability to trust since she was still an extremely frightened young horse. Some even considered her a wild horse.

Solemn trotted in a looping chain of circles, constantly keeping a watchful eye on the girl in the center. A girl who needed so much to be accepted exactly how she was, waiting to become all that she was created to be.

Knowing glances drifted between Emily and Solemn. They had lived deeply similar lives. Had shared the same crushing blows of rejection, isolation, and loneliness. Understanding began to occur on a level deeper than words.

With a subtleness that only a trained eye could see, the filly's perfect circling began to falter, drifting into irregular patterns. Her eyes shifted from a wary measuring of Emily to a soft invitation. The invitation melted into a voiceless plea.

Like an electrical conduit the silence between them was alive with communication. They seemed to be looking into each other's hearts, finding there a reflection of themselves. Through their pain they reached toward each other—girl to horse, hand to hide. Abruptly the filly turned in to the center of the ring, slowing to a walk that brought her within inches of Emily and me.

"Oh my gosh!" Sondra gasped, moving her hands reactively toward her face. She knew Solemn's background, her mistrust of people. Balancing between unbelief and amazement, Sondra obviously understood the impact of this moment. I backed silently out of the pen, leaving Emily and Solemn alone together.

Neither wished to be alone again. Standing nose to nose, black filly to blond girl, they complemented each other like salt and pepper, like night and day, each filling a void within the other.

Sondra gripped the top of the gate in white-knuckle fashion, watching this sudden flowering of her child's soul. With the softness of a dove, Emily placed her hand on Solemn's forehead and began to rub it in slow circles.

With her other hand she cupped the filly's cheeks and kissed her velvety muzzle.

A barely audible giggle broke from Emily's lips. I glanced at her mother. Sondra's eyes glistened; tears left silver traces down her cheeks.

From behind the solid wall of the round pen, I asked Emily to turn and walk away from Solemn. I wanted her to know that the filly had approached her willingly and deliberately. I wanted her to know this was no coincidence.

Reluctantly, not wanting to leave the warmth of this tentative new friendship, Emily did as I asked. After taking a dozen steps, she stopped. A black muzzle gently bumped her in the back. Instant realization split her face into a smile that would have melted steel. "Mom!" she cried—it was the only shocked word that escaped her lips. But it clearly captured her transparent joy.

Sondra watched it all in slack-jawed amazement—the outcast horse choosing to follow the outcast girl. The process was repeated several times. Finally, Emily turned back around and stepped into the filly's space. Lifting her arms, she encircled Solemn's neck with a full embrace, resting her cheek against the filly's.

From the gate, Sondra dropped her forehead onto the backs of her hands and wept openly. For mother and daughter walls of sorrow came crashing down under a roaring flood of release.

I looked from girl to horse. Emily's eyes were peacefully closed, the filly's dreamily half open. The two leaned into each other, resting, drawing comfort from one another. Cheek to cheek, their posture embodied a silent, healing promise. Between the two of them it became their Solemn vow.

Fast Forward

∽

KIDS HAVE AN innate sense of when to kiss what needs kissing and when to hug what needs hugging.

Matthew and I had just brought out his favorite horse, an Appaloosa mare called Jasmine. At fourteen and a half hands and sixteen years old, I thought she was the perfect size and temperament for this busy six-year-old boy. Matthew could fit more life into a minute than others could in an afternoon.

Together we groomed her through a hail of machine gun paced questions. Matthew tackled each task with complete fervor and passion. He moved and talked with twice the speed of a mortal being. The simple act of cleaning out a hoof quickly escalated into full combat with an imaginary foe. The hoof pick suddenly turned into a miraculous device that vaporized the enemy. Of course, the entire scene was furnished with lifelike sound effects.

Just being with Matthew was like standing near a waterfall. Without realizing it, his zest for life would cover me like a fine mist. Before long I was drenched with the pure life that literally sloshed and splashed from his magnificent wake.

Matthew could draw any adult to shed grown-up boundaries and live like a child again. Why walk when you can run? Why talk when you can shout? Why stroll through the grass when you can roll through it? There's just so much life to experience.

Once the grooming was finished, we practically ran to the tack room. I handed Matthew the bridle while I reached around for a small saddle.

The ranch was in full swing, and I suddenly found myself momentarily trapped in the corner by mingling leaders and children. When I was able, I made my way to the door with saddle, pad, and helmet draped over my arm. While striding across the small porch I glanced up—a speeding train would not have stopped me faster!

Matthew was under Jasmine and appeared to have his head upside down and stuck between her front legs! His little body was crouching directly beneath her girth. His tiny chest was pressed against the space just behind her front legs, with each arm extended out and up toward her back.

Blessed Jasmine was peacefully taking it all in stride as I cautiously approached them. "Matthew, honey, are you all right?" I asked with a calming voice.

He rotated his head to the right, which placed his left ear firmly between her pectoral muscles. With dreamy eyes veiled by Cupid's arrow, he looked up at me and proclaimed, "I just *love* her!"

"Oh my gosh, you're giving Jasmine a hug!" I suddenly realized out loud. Now his contorted posture made perfect sense. After all, that's how you would hug your mom, chest to chest, with arms wrapped around her body.

"That's so sweet," I crooned while gently grasping his wrist and pulling him out from under the patient freckled gray mare.

After safely guiding Matthew to the velvety space between her nostrils, I redirected his affection by saying with a laugh, "I think she needs a kiss now!"

The Negotiator

❦

THE DAY SHE arrived at the ranch, everyone did their best not to shrink back from the black filly we had just rescued. Not only was Solemn's physical condition hideous, her sheer terror of humans made her impossible to approach. Eventually, one by one, the "Good Samaritans" who had tried to be kind to her would give up and leave their offerings of carrots or grain on the ground before walking away. All but one, that is. All but Sierra.

Sierra was drawn toward the skeletal filly like a sunflower to sunlight. I told her the filly's background, and she devoured every detail until I said that there were other horses that had been left behind. Perhaps more than twenty others were still trapped in hopelessness. She heard nothing else—that one fact pierced her heart like an arrow of ice.

I learned later that Sierra, who normally takes every day by the tail, quietly retreated that evening to the privacy of her bedroom. Only there, alone at last, did she allow her grieving heart to spill out a torrent of compassionate tears.

Within days, Sierra begged me for any photographs I had of the other horses who might still be suffering. She could barely eat or sleep, knowing there were other horses needing to be rescued. Finally she told me her simple plan. With all the tender wisdom of her fourteen years, she said, "I've been saving up to buy a saddle. Maybe...just maybe it will be enough."

It had taken her over a year to earn that money.

If she could gain the approval of her parents, Sierra hoped to use her savings to purchase the release of one of the other suffering horses. She understood that her family's "financial strain meter" was already in the red zone and that owning a large animal would only increase that strain.

Sierra talked with her dad and laid out the contents of her heart like a map, looking solely to him for guidance. After presenting her case, she wordlessly handed him the photographs. One by one, he went through them. Soundless minutes passed slowly as he absorbed each pitiful image.

Sierra watched as his compassionate eyes began to fill with tears. More long moments passed. Finally, in a voice that was soft and hoarse, he spoke. "Honey, I am so proud of you." He cleared his throat. "You put the greater need of one of God's creatures ahead of your own. You could have spent this money on a hundred different things— things that *you* need. But instead, you want to give it for another's need. You make me proud to be your dad."

The last Saturday in June was our annual tack sale and horse fair—a day of fun and fundraising for the ranch. Thanks to the dedication of our staff and many volunteers, it blossomed into an outstanding event. All of us from the ranch were overwhelmed and at the same time humbled to experience the generosity of our community as people gave of themselves and their time to help us out. We met so many incredible people and made dozens of new friends.

One kindhearted cowboy, with a reputation for excellence and safety in his horse transportation business, donated for our raffle the use of his deluxe six-horse trailer and his services for a long-distance transport job. Many of the thousands attending the fair purchased raffle tickets, hoping to win the free service. At four o'clock the winning ticket was drawn and announced.

The winner had already gone home, so I had the great pleasure of telephoning her to relay the good news. The phone rang and rang. I hoped I wouldn't get the answering machine.

At last a young voice answered, and I blurted out, "You won! Sierra, you won the horse transport!" I could hear her squealing excitedly on the other end, and I went on, "I think the Lord is bumping your backside to carry out your rescue plans. Let's make a date...."

Within days all of the necessary arrangements had been made. Sierra's adventure would begin in two weeks.

During the interim, Sierra shared her dream with many of her friends. On the morning of our scheduled rendezvous a dozen other kids showed up, all wishing to accompany us on the trip. Some were coming to lend their support. Others carried cash in their pockets and hoped to follow Sierra's courageous lead.

From the rising dream of one, a small army had formed behind her to make a difference in any way they could. Without meaning to, Sierra had become a leader of active selflessness for her peers to follow.

We set out together in a caravan led by our new friends

who were donating their time and skills in driving the horse trailer. After traveling a good distance, we all stopped at a rest area on a mountain pass.

Once again I firmly reminded our entourage that they were about to see some devastating things. I warned them not to cry, scream, or act out in any way, no matter how bad it was. I cautioned them that if they couldn't bear it, to quietly walk away and shed their tears in private. "Our host needs our utmost kindness and respect," I added. I knew that any judgmental or emotional behavior would not enhance our ability to negotiate the release of desperate horses.

With somber expressions everyone nodded in acknowledgment of what I'd said. I watched as they steeled their young hearts against the unknown that lay ahead. In silence we climbed back into our vehicles and set off on the last leg of the journey.

The kids were remarkably brave and kind. We wandered through the scattered corrals of the rundown ranch with little groups breaking away from time to time, only to return with freshly dried cheeks and newly squared shoulders. Even after viewing gut-wrenching scenes, the girls handled each situation with professionalism and courtesy.

After looking over the horses that were for sale, the kids drew back into a little conference. In an orderly fashion they determined which animals were in the greatest need and discussed what kind of financial offer might be accepted.

Several of us adults stood by only to help facilitate the girls' decision. None of them had enough money individually to make a difference. But I watched in awe as these children came together and like flints striking against the steel in each other, combined their sparks to create a fire! By pooling every nickel, dime, and dollar, they had enough financial power to unlock the prison doors for at least some of the horses. They proposed to offer the ranch owner a package deal, and with a little junior high persuasion their offer was accepted.

They did it! At the end of that emotionally-charged, exhausting day, the horse trailer pulled away from that distant rundown ranch with four horses inside. This amazing feat was not executed by law enforcement, a group of outraged adults, or by any animal rights organization. It was accomplished by a handful of little girls.

All because one ordinary girl believed that she could make a difference.

Southbound

〜⚮〜

BENEATH A SUN-BAKED sky, I lifted my damp hat and wiped my forehead. The humid fragrance of the hay field rose to permeate all my senses. Rewarding myself with a deep breath, I quickly replaced my hat and heaved the freshly birthed hay bale up onto the meandering flatbed.

With straining biceps and aching low back, I gazed at the nearly eternal serpentine of bales still to be moved off the field.

Powdery green dust hung inside the barn, making prickly paste on my wet skin. No time to scratch as the impatient hay conveyer chugged and clattered an endless train of bales toward calloused hands. Dusk was overcome by twilight. Stars began to twinkle on the eastern horizon. The hay conveyor rattled on into the night.

Dawn poured over the land in a butter-colored wave. Worn hands lifted newly stacked bales into the hay cart to be ferried to each hungry mouth. Nickering gave way to munching contentment as each equine soul found solace in the new grass hay. One chore done, another to begin.

With manure cart and fork in hand I contemplated one of the great mysteries in my life. The age-old question taunted my tired brain as I shoveled up pile after pile of metabolized hay. I stood up straight and surveyed my surroundings. Like gathered smooth stones from a dry creek bed, manure lay stacked in infinite, giggling monuments beneath the early morning sun.

In dumbfounded silence I shook my head. The rationale of simple math and physics blew away in the morning breeze. Once again I asked myself, "How can you feed a horse one ton of hay...and know that the south end will make three?"

hope

rising

like the

evening star

Miracle

W·ITHOUT A spoken word, Jennifer's eyes alone told her story. Standing beside her loving mother, she seemed too destroyed to even look at me. When she found the courage to lift her eyes, it was for only an instant. It was not unlike seeing the flash of a falling star. In the split second that her eyes met mine, what I saw chilled me to the bone.

I saw absolute, stunning beauty veiled in hollow, bleeding sorrow. A tiny flame trapped in an icy prison. How could two elements so dichotomous be found in the same place? Her deep blue eyes were magnificently etched with radiating white lines like a star burst. Maybe in another time they would have looked very much like sparkles dancing on the surface of sapphire waters. Now, curtained in sorrow, they looked like nothing other than shattered glass.

Those deep blue shards silently communicated unspeakable pain, anguish, and rejection. Her fourteen years of brutal multileveled abuse had driven her to near destruction. Implosion appeared to be imminent. In one flickering instant I witnessed pain so great that it nearly knocked me backward. *Lord, this child needs a miracle,* I prayed.

Five months passed, and I was still no closer to having

anything that resembled a conversation with Jennifer. The crushing weight of her daily avalanche of despair was taking a heavy toll. She was so deep inside herself that her few words came out one at a time as though they had to be hauled up like stranded rock climbers from the bleak cavern of her soul.

I called her often on the phone, but it was so difficult to know if I had spoken too much or too little. Did she feel pressured to talk? Was I overwhelming her with words? Did she feel pestered instead of loved? Usually after hanging up the phone, I felt frustrated that I couldn't be what she needed. Was I just one more person in a long line of others who had failed her miserably?

On one particularly cold November day, Jennifer was riding Dove, a chestnut pinto mare, around the arena. Through the ebbing light I watched her intently. On this day, Jennifer was especially somber. Her sorrow was like a living thing, crawling across the space between us, tearing at my heart. Stupidly I asked, "How was your day today?"

After a long while, lifting her gaze from the dust, she simply shook her head and mouthed, "Not good."

I motioned for her to ride into the center of the arena and meet me so we could talk privately. She brought Dove to a halt, and I put my hand on her knee and looked up into her face. "Honey, what happened?"

She averted her eyes, struggling to voice her thoughts. When at last she did speak, the words were like a rain of broken glass falling on my face and shoulders. "Today at school a group of kids knocked me to the ground." Jennifer's voice was barely loud enough to be heard above the background chatter of other kids riding nearby. "They took turns hitting me and throwing dirt on my head. They

were laughing.... They tried to outdo each other, calling
me awful names." Her voice dropped even lower. "Finally
someone scratched one of those names into my back with
a pin," she whispered.

Behind us even the fading sunlight seemed too weak to
bear this sorrow and quietly bowed below the horizon.
Gray darkness crept over the land as together our silent
tears slipped to the earth. I reached up and for the first
time, Jennifer reached down to me. The little pinto stood
quietly as I held the weeping girl against me.

We walked quietly for a while, side by side. The violet
twilight gave way to darkness. And there in front of us on
the horizon rose the first evening star.

A month later I stood looking up at Jennifer again.
This time she was sitting astride one of our most magnificent horses, my own mare, Ele. It had been an easy
decision to choose Jennifer as the center attraction of our
ranch's entry into the town's Christmas parade. She and
Ele were completely draped in shimmering red fabric that
was adorned with sparkling tinsel and garlands. Rubies
would have paled in brilliance next to them. Every breath
of wind fluttered their costume in waves of radiant crim-
son. In keeping with the "Christmas gift" theme of our
ten horse-and-rider teams in the parade, Jennifer, Ele,
and I were decorated to represent the "gift of love." It
seemed appropriate since Jennifer had known so much of
the opposite in her short life.

While waiting for our turn to enter the parade route,
several passing people saw Jennifer, stopped short, and
began photographing her. I smiled up at her. "See, you're
so beautiful they can't help but take your picture!" She
responded nervously with a weak little upturn of her lips.

Finally it was our turn to step forward into the jubilant fray. Our ten brilliantly decorated horses moved ahead, patiently allowing themselves to be led while carrying a costumed rider, surrounded by a glittering entourage of five or more vibrantly dressed children.

Jennifer's job—the job of all the children in our group—was to make as many people smile as possible. I set out leading Ele down the parade route, and I looked up at Jennifer to remind her to smile and wave.

Immediately I realized that would be difficult for her—she looked like a newborn fawn frozen silent and stiff by sheer terror. *One step at a time,* I thought.

After about a quarter of a mile, I noticed that one of Jennifer's hands had left the security of the reins and was making a hesitant attempt at waving. My heart smiled.

By the time the parade began to turn into the center of town, the crowd had grown to thousands. People stood ten or more deep on both sides of us. Floats and horses meandered down the main street, a multicolored, glistening river between banks of cheering children, men, and women.

In the midst of all the noise of the celebration I thought I heard a single small voice. *Yes! There it was again.* Barely audible but definite.

"Merry Christmas," Jennifer breathed to the crowd. And then louder. "Merry Christmas!"

I looked up to see my "gift of love" waving broadly. She met my glance with a huge smile. It was the first time I had ever seen her teeth! Her smile was like a shaft of sunlight, melting the icy chill that had gripped me since I first looked into her tormented eyes. A laser beam to my heart would have had less impact! The tiny spark that had survived deep inside Jennifer suddenly burst into healing flames. Repressed hope surged to the surface of her soul. Pure joy came pouring out like a white hot fire.

The happy commotion around us seemed suddenly muted, a distant background din underneath Jennifer's triumphant shouts to the onlookers. It became one of those golden days in my life.

Jennifer had chosen to break through the ice of adversity. I instated her as a junior leader in the daily operations of our ranch, and she continued to grow in every way. Like many girls her age she battled against her sense of insecurity, low self-esteem, and shyness. But she worked hard to conquer those strongholds in her life.

Day by day, step by step, Jennifer grew stronger until finally a newfound sense of confidence emerged the victor. She began to lead the way by hugging others first. Over the following summer she tended to the needs of younger children by making them feel loved and accepted. She even helped teach a junior leader class. I quietly watched as she moved from project to project to help make our ranch a better place. By choosing to allow her anguish to make her stronger, Jennifer soared above what used to be a painful horizon. Now, within a heart full of hope, her evening star had risen.

On a hot September day in her quiet way, Jennifer said, "I think it's time." We had talked often about her dream of having a horse of her own. Now I produced a pen and a pad of paper, and we sat down on the tack room porch to compile a list of what she would need and what it would cost.

By the time we had written down every item, the total came to more than two thousand dollars—without the horse! For Jennifer and her single mother, trying to come up with that kind of money would be like walking on water. Believing it could be possible was a Herculean step of faith.

She needed a miracle.

I told Jennifer to pray about it. "If it's meant to be," I said, "it will happen in God's timing."

Jennifer began calling me every night to give an account of the day's miraculous happenings. A family friend had an old English saddle that they were willing to part with. Another friend donated a headstall, reins, and several bits, and then one of her relatives found an old box of grooming equipment in their garage. In only one week, Jennifer had accumulated every item on the list!

All that was left to complete her dream was a horse. Just for fun I asked her, "If money had nothing to do with it, what kind of a horse would you choose?"

She stammered for a moment. It seemed difficult for her to open the door of her imagination and allow her dreams to fly free. She would have been happy with anything that had four legs and a beating heart. But she slowly rose to the challenge and began to envision her dream horse. "If I could choose anything—" her eyes rolled skyward—"I would choose a horse like yours. Like Ele. Someday I'd like to learn dressage and maybe even show in English or hunt seat." Absently, deep in thought, she rested her chin in one cupped hand. "I think I would really like a thoroughbred—maybe a gelding...no, a mare. Definitely a mare. It would be great if she were tall...maybe sixteen hands."

"As long as we're dreaming," I said with a grin, "let's dream in color."

"Hmm...black, or maybe bay. I've always liked bays,"

she added, with a distant, upward gaze. She was caught in the act of daring to imagine the perfect horse for her. After a long moment, she returned to reality and looked at me with a smile. Her dream was coming to life through words. I hoped she felt as good about it as I did.

Our equine rescue operation is well known now in our area, and the ranch receives frequent calls from people wanting to donate horses to our program or to adoptive families. Nearly all of these horses have special needs. They are either very young or too old to have much "useful" life left. Often they are physically broken down or have dangerous behavioral problems. Few people donate sound horses because sound horses can be sold.

I received one of these calls five days after Jennifer's "perfect horse daydream." The woman's voice told me how her daughter had shown this mare for several years, but had now moved on to a horse that could compete at a higher level. We had a pleasant chat while I dug out my adoption-placement notebook to take down her name and number.

Then I began my usual list of questions. "What type of showing did your daughter do?"

"Mostly hunt seat," the woman replied. "The horse is a class A-B show horse. She has no bad habits and is completely sound."

I sat up straight, hope rising in my heart. "What else can you tell me about her?"

"She's twelve years old and easily sixteen hands."

Excitement nearly overtook my ability to write! Mentally I was going down Jennifer's dream list: Show horse—check. Thoroughbred—check. Mare—check. Sixteen hands—check.... I had to ask. "I know this is a ridiculous question, but could you tell me what color she is?" I could feel my nose wrinkle as I closed my eyes tightly.

"Why, she's a black bay," she said matter-of-factly.

"*Yes!*" I all but shouted as I shot up, knocking my chair over backward. I picked it up, laughing, and said breathlessly, "How does it feel to be a child's answer to prayer?"

A star rising through darkness. A spark igniting into flame. A broken heart gaining strength. A distant wish finding wings. A dream coming true. These had become Jennifer's stepping stones of gold in her miraculous journey across her sea of despair.

Her sapphire eyes, with the white crackles that had once reminded me of broken glass, now sparkled like brilliant star bursts. Looking at Jennifer's shining joy as she pressed her soft pale cheek gently against her mare's soft dark cheek, a friend asked, "What's your new horse's name?"

With an enormous flashing smile, in appreciation of the One who answered her prayers, she simply said, "Her name is...Miracle."

Force of One

_My_ LIFE IS SO completely
blessed by a myriad of special friends. Each one is unique
and separate, embodying an individual beauty. Like
embracing a magnificent bouquet of flowers, each single
masterpiece carries with it a fragrance that is unequaled.

Such is Katie, a rare blossom who constantly exempli-
fies how beautiful a heart can be when it is deeply rooted
in the rich soil of selflessness. Katie has taught me on several occasions the beauty of simply giving from where your
roots have spread. To her, generosity is one of the most
natural things a heart can know.

While I struggle with the foreign entanglements of
fundraising and what might work and what hasn't, she
simply does it. With the apparent ease of breathing, Katie
intrinsically knows how to gather finances for the things
that she believes in. She doesn't sweat or struggle, beat a
drum or ring a bell. Endowed with a quiet confidence, she
has learned how to clear a space beneath her flourishing
leaves and encourage good will to grow up beside her.

Katie has allowed the normal events of her life to
channel help where help is needed. She does innocuous
things such as having a concession stand at her own birth-

day celebration. Katie informed her guests that all of the proceeds would be donated to the charity of her choice.

Without telling anyone she consolidated all her monetary Christmas gifts. Instead of spending the money on herself, she quietly mailed her gifts off to our ranch to help support horses she barely knows.

To say that Katie's acts of kindness have humbled me down to the very core of my soul would reveal only a fraction of how much she has actually moved me. I have learned so much from her already. She is definitely an example of what one committed heart can do. Katie constantly reminds me that she is, as anyone *can* be, truly a force of one.

And all this from someone who has experienced the ranch only once, lives hundreds of miles away...and is only eleven years old.

Dumb Farm Animals?

❧

UNDER THE bright yellow glare of a naked lightbulb, the chestnut gelding stood trembling and groaning in pain. He was crashing fast from a severe case of colic.

Colic, a condition that all horse owners fear, is caused by impaction or blockage in the bowel. The ailment has many origins—a sudden change of diet or weather, stress, too much rich grass, moldy or tainted feed, a foreign object...the list goes on and on. Even though horses are known for their strength and stamina, their digestive systems are remarkably fragile. Horses cannot vomit, so whatever they eat must pass through the entire length of their digestive tract—about a hundred feet of intestines with many tight twists and turns.

Some colics are so mild that they can be remedied simply by keeping the horse walking. Others can be so severe that death comes almost immediately, or the horse writhes in agony—sometimes for days—until its bowels finally rupture, and it collapses in death.

Like cancer in humans, colic in horses is not always

fatal, but it is always feared. Surgical options for severely colicky horses are not only excruciatingly painful, but also prohibitively expensive with an often poor prognosis. Of the available options, we had decided to treat our stricken horse Quincy by literally flooding him with intravenous fluids in the hope that the blockage would be saturated into a form that the horse could pass from his system.

Troy, Sarah, and I hastily converted a stall into a makeshift hospital room, loosely tying Quincy in the corner. Above his head we hammered up temporary hooks to hold the bags of intravenous fluids he needed. Catheterization tubes jutted out of veins on each side of his neck. The leads were fully open, allowing a virtual river of fluids to flow uninterrupted into each thumb-sized vein.

An aching cold fog had settled around us, forming a pristine inch-thick layer of intricate lacy ice crystals on every surface. It's easy to appreciate this white wonder— some of nature's finest artwork—from the warmth of the house. It's quite another thing to experience firsthand how needle-sharp the brutal teeth of winter can be.

The penetrating cold was beginning to freeze the IV fluid within the coils of tubing before it could reach our ailing horse. We set up a kerosene heater to keep the fluid flowing and to warm our sick friend.

The five-liter IV bags were emptying into Quincy's veins at the rate of a bag every fifteen to twenty minutes. We could only watch helplessly as he shuddered and groaned with each painful contraction of his gut.

With cold fluid flowing into his body at an exponential rate, Quincy soon began to shiver violently. In our desperate effort to maintain his body heat, we wrapped the suffering gelding in three full-size body blankets and then topped those with a heavy-duty sleeping bag. Then we hustled up the hill to our house with twenty bags or more of the IV fluids—about twenty-five gallons—and put them into the hot tub to warm up.

Once that was done, there was little else to do but wait. Minutes ticked by into the early hours of the morning. And then we began to witness something completely unexpected.

The door from Quincy's "hospital" stall led into the main corral where most of our riding herd lives. We watched in amazement as, one by one, at twenty-minute intervals, almost every horse in the corral came to visit Quincy.

Our massive draft horse, Luke, Quincy's main play-mate, was the first to offer his sympathy and support. Extending his magnificent neck as far as he could, he reached deeply into his ailing buddy's stall, gently massaging Quincy's rump and tail with his lips. At times when Quincy groaned in pain, Luke nickered in a voice so low that it could scarcely be heard.

Troy, Sarah, and I met each other's wide eyes and said nothing.

River, a bay Arab gelding, was the next to reach in for a visit. He was so small that he had to stand with all of his feet together to reach into the stall. From time to time, he rested his chin on top of his sick friend's tail.

Throughout our watches during that bitter night, each of us grew more intrigued as horse after horse came to give their special brand of support to their stricken friend. It was as though even these "dumb farm animals," as they are so often called, knew the healing value of love.

Troy took the graveyard shift. In a futile attempt to ward off the cold, he made a cocoon of horse blankets and a sleeping bag, burrowing under this during the fifteen-minute intervals between hanging IV bags.

The cold grew so intense that he finally hammered up a horse blanket over the opening behind Quincy's rump, trying to seal in as much heat as possible. The night ticked on, one frozen minute at a time.

The next morning I layered on most of the coats I owned, bracing myself for the biting cold. I opened the front door and stepped out into the white rush of bone-chilling winter. Earth, sky, and everything in between lay in a frozen milky haze, embalmed under a thick layer of shimmering white filigree.

I was surprised, when the barn came into view through the fog, that the horses weren't gathered around the gate as they always were, pacing about in anticipation of their breakfast. Instead, they were huddled, football-team fashion, around the blanketed opening into their sick friend's stall.

I wouldn't have believed it if I hadn't seen it for myself. Concern for Quincy was seemingly more important than meeting their own need for food. It wasn't until I wheeled their breakfast bales of hay through the main gate that our herd began to break away from their supportive huddle.

Sarah and I took up the dayshift with Quincy. The bitter cold wore on. From time to time we pulled back the tacked-up blanket and watched the clockwork rotation as our equine family continued to comfort their sick companion.

The horses kept coming, twenty-four hours a day...for four days.

By the fourth day, Troy, Sarah, and I were utterly exhausted. And we knew that Quincy would soon either pass his blockage—or he would die.

In the middle of the day, a small procession of visiting kids who had heard about Quincy's plight quietly entered the barn. One at a time, in much the same way as the horses in the corral, the children came and comforted our sick gelding. One small boy simply buried his face against Quincy's shoulder and cried. With a tiny voice meant only for his four-legged pal, I overheard him plead, "Please don't die…please don't die."

After all the kids had their turn at Quincy's side, they wanted to pray for him. With faith as solid as the earth beneath their feet, they reached out for each other's hands and laced fingers. The simple prayer that followed would have moved any mountain of the Cascade Range.

Later that afternoon a glimmer of hope shattered the gloom around us. Quincy's gut began to roil and churn in noisy proclamations. Movement! Something inside was moving! With each rumbling growl, Sarah's eyebrows shot upward. Hesitant grins split our faces.

Nearly simultaneously the flooded gelding began to urinate. He continued to relieve himself of enormous amounts of fluid every few minutes.

Then came the unabashed herald of what he had been pushing against for the last four days—he flatulated!

"Wahoo!" Sarah and I both cheered and spun a victory dance in the barn. With Quincy's every root and toot we laughed out loud. Surely angels must have been splitting their sides in laughter over how excited these two girls were over a horse passing gas!

Within the hour the gelding's hind end turned into a weapon of mass destruction. Nothing within eight feet was safe from the onslaught. Never in all my life have I ever been so thrilled to see a horse have explosive diarrhea!

By nightfall, Quincy was casually eating and drinking and passing normal manure. The crisis was over. But after administering volumes of pain medications and hanging 157 liters of intravenous fluids, I still believe that it took more than just medicine to heal him. Through all the torment of his illness I believe that his will to keep fighting was fueled by the love and compassion so diligently administered by his equine family. In his time of need he was never alone. As his strength failed, their strength prevailed. I am equally convinced that the loving devotion and prayers of his little fan club played a major role in pulling him back from the brink of death.

The next morning, with great relief, I released Quincy back into the main corral. Each horse, as if their hearts were metallic and he was magnetic north, rotated to face him. Silently, with ears and eyes forward, they came to him in what looked like a protective circle. They investigated Quincy's entire body, giving special attention to his nostrils and the shaved areas of his neck that still bore the wounds from his being catheterized.

While I watched Quincy's warm reception back into the herd, I couldn't help but think the scene felt strangely familiar. And then the nearly forgotten memory came flooding back. There I was in my third grade class, experiencing a similar examination.

I had been out of school for a week following a "Wide World of Sports"-style crash that had left me with twenty-eight stitches in my lip and chin. The day I came back to class there was such a commotion that the teacher finally gave up and allowed the entire class to surround me.

Like a little tomboy put on display for a visiting aunt, I slowly rotated for them all. "Does it hurt?" they asked. "Wow! How many stitches is that?" "Can I touch it?" "Are you okay?" "Does that go all the way through your lip?" "When do you get them out?"

And finally, "We're glad you're back. We missed you."

I couldn't help but wonder, watching the horses welcome Quincy back to the corral, if the gelding was the recipient of such inquisitive kindness and support. It certainly looked like it. I closed the corral gate behind me and said with a chuckle, "Dumb farm animals? Too bad we're not all so dumb."

A Warm Handshake

I T WAS THE end of a very hot
and dusty day. The walk up the hill from the ranch common yard toward our home seemed especially long.
Before entering the house, I pulled off my boots and
brushed the afternoon dust off my pants. Our guests were
already arriving for the evening. We host a weekly group
that joins together for dinner, a few songs, and a simple
Bible teaching from Troy. The sense of family among the
group feels as welcome as a heartbeat.

Everyone there knows that it's a time when the broken
find healing, the weak find support, and the joyful scatter
gifts like seeds of pure gold. When we join together as a
team, a family, our feeble hands become strong. It is our
favorite time of the week.

After saying grace and releasing hands, hungry fingers
quickly found their way into every bowl. My little kitchen
was filled with dusty bodies bumping and milling about,
assisting each other in filling their plates. Above the giggling chaos the phone rang. I navigated the crowd like a
bumper car, with a half-eaten baked potato in hand, until
I finally reached for the receiver.

It was Ray, Elishah's father. Even though I didn't know

him well, I could immediately tell that his easygoing rancher's style was somehow tightened. Our brief conversation revealed that he had injured his back and was in a great deal of pain. To make matters worse, he had been baling hay at the time. "Can you please send Elishah home to help bring in the hay?" he said through lips that sounded drawn with pain.

"How much hay is down?" I asked while covering my ear to better hear him. "It's a small field," he said, and then I heard him tallying to himself. "Maybe two to three hundred bales." I glanced at Elishah through the hungry, jostling group. Although she is known to us all as a five-foot-one-inch package of pure ranch-bred, rocket-fueled *try hard*, the task was far greater than even she could manage.

My heart began to twist with conflict. I would love to help, but...I glanced around my home at kids and leaders just settling down with paper plates full of supper balanced on their knees. The dinner had already started, and our time together would last until nearly dark.

My gaze lingered on the group. All these folks had come for fellowship, for ministry, for something that would fill their hearts. Then lightning flashed across my tired brain: True happiness is not found in gaining what we don't have, but in giving what we do. The greatest joy, the greatest peace, the greatest fulfillment within this life is giving what we have, not seeking what we *want*. If this young group truly sought fulfillment, this might be their answer. Abruptly I told Ray that I would call him right back.

I called for everyone's attention and shared Ray's plight. Without hesitation the kids agreed wholeheartedly to my proposed solution. With deep gratitude, Elishah called her father back and simply said, "Don't worry, Dad; help is on the way."

Dinner and plates were left on the kitchen counter as everyone began to ready themselves for the task at hand. My husband, Troy, led the charge as kids grabbed hats, gloves, and long-sleeved shirts from the coatrack in the living room, while filing out the front door. Everyone piled into trucks as we made a hasty caravan over the handful of miles that separated Ray's ranch from ours.

Upon arrival the kids pulled on their gloves and followed the sound of Ray's baler chugging through the pasture. Like geese in flight the kids ran ahead of the hay truck as it bumped and jerked through the field. That team ferried the hay to the other team of kids on the flatbed, who neatly stacked the endless stream of bales that was being tossed at their feet. Through the eyes of any rancher it was poetry in motion.

I hefted bale after bale onto the groaning flatbed, and I couldn't help but think of my grandmother. The memory made me smile. I knew she would call this "a warm handshake." That was her version of giving someone what they needed beyond what they could do for themselves.

The sun balanced on the horizon, suspended in radiant agreement with the day's work. The field lay washed in soft shafts of orange and yellow light. The tumbling contentment of a nearby stream rose gently to join in the evening chorus of the gathering nighthawks. All life seemed to be celebrating the precious gift of one more day.

I watched the kids, running and laughing through this simple place, a rolling hay field. It seemed as if every step on the fresh cut pasture released a humid wave of grassy perfume, rich with the fragrance of summer. Yet when bathed in the molten colors of twilight, wafting with the warm fragrance of life, it could have been heaven itself.

After tucking the last load of hay into the barn, the young, benevolent group walked back up to the inviting red ranch house. To everyone's surprise, Elishah's mother had waiting a checker-clothed table laden with fresh-baked pies, ice cream, and glass pitchers brimming with sweet mint tea.

Damp from the efforts of the evening, the kids exchanged wet hugs among the group. With contented fatigue and a plate full of pie, they spread out beneath a sprawling tree whose branches were strung with soft yellow bulbs.

I leaned back on an old wooden bench with a tall glass of icy tea and watched these young ones with deep satisfaction. I thought to myself, *This is fellowship. Ministry is not confined to a place or a thing—it is who we are. It is what we do with our heart and our hands. It is everything that we choose to give.*

Above the yellow glow of the lights beyond the dark branches of the trees, as if in agreement, a nighthawk's song filled the twilight.

hope
rising
triumphant

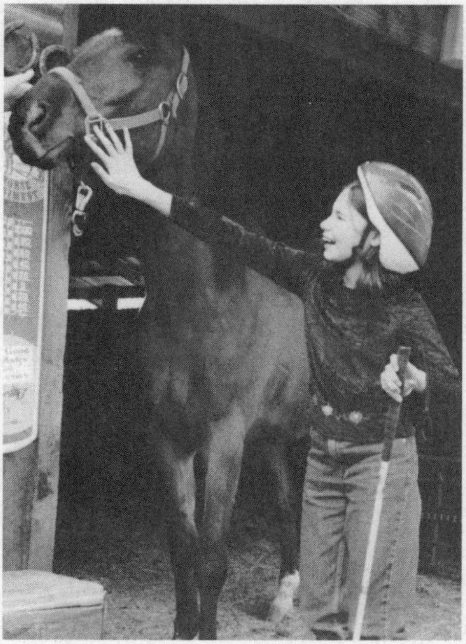

Hurdles of Life

ЄACH FALL, as the hum of ranch activity begins to subside, I take a moment to reflect on the season just past. This last season felt as if the entire time was spent running hurdles. I tried to soar over the first one, take a few strides, and then reach for the next one as best I could. But soon after there came another...and another, until they were coming so close together that there was no time to gain strength between leaps.

By the end of the summer I feared my form was more like that of a charging rhino than a graceful hurdler. I was off my stride and had crashed through more hurdles than I had sailed over. Some races are just like that. Each month of last season came with the usual load of normal hurdles expected with running a large ranching program. Unfortunately there were many more that weren't anticipated. This was my view of looking down the track....

APRIL

Several organizations in the States rescue neglected and abused horses, as we do, and pair them with physically and emotionally needy children. What sets our ranch apart is the intensely personal nature of our program—one child with one horse and one counselor, 100 percent of the time. Every child, every time they come to the ranch, has the complete, loving attention of a leader. This translates into a dynamic, open-ended session, lasting from an hour to an entire afternoon, enabling the child to deal with whatever he or she is facing at the time.

Our "children"—from toddlers to grandparents—come from every socioeconomic level. Troy and I determined when we founded Crystal Peaks that our programs would be equally available to all, so we never charge a fee. We provide for our four to five thousand visitors each season along with twenty-five horses and our support staff, which requires creative financing. The needs of the ranch have usually been met through generous private donations, fund-raising, and some grants. However, as any nonprofit organization can attest, there are seasons of plenty...and seasons of lack.

Such was the month of April.

Financial reserves had dipped into the red. Our hay supply alone was dwindling faster than our income could replace it. Without help we would run out within the month.

We were eagerly anticipating the approval of several "ringer" grants—grants we were certain to receive because our operation exactly matched the required criteria. The next two weeks brought more bad news—our grants were turned down, and private donations all but disappeared. Troy and I started paying ranch expenses with our savings.

It was only a matter of time before we would have to walk through our herd—our family—and choose the horses that must be sold....

MAY

Everyone who spends time around horses runs the risk of being hurt by them. Even riding a bicycle has its risks. But a bicycle is only metal and rubber. It can't think for itself. A horse, on the other hand, is a thousand-pound living creature that reacts instinctively and survives by fleeing danger. All too often when injuries occur, the rider blames the horse because he is too embarrassed or arrogant to admit that he put himself and the horse in a bad situation that ended with a bad result.

It's my job as director of the ranch to pair children who usually know nothing about horses with horses that often know nothing about children. At best it is a tenuous balance. Parents entrust us with their most priceless gifts— their children. It's our responsibility to keep them safe while they are in our care.

My staff and I have always worked hard to provide the safest environment possible. Over twenty thousand kids have ridden at Crystal Peaks since we opened, yet we have never had one serious injury. Through much hard work and just as much prayer, we're thankful that we've never experienced more than our share of bumps and bruises.

But the risk is always present. And in May my greatest fear was realized.

From the moment she came to Crystal Peaks, Jenie completely captured my heart with her vivacious spirit. A college student with a strong background in youth ministries, this blond, blue-eyed beauty was also an experienced horsewoman who had competed at high levels in jumping and hunt seat. We walked together around the corrals, talking of all the possibilities to come, and I felt humbled and blessed that such a dynamic young woman was joining my senior staff.

Only the day before, we had rescued two starving Arabian colts. They were in pitiful condition, and, as we usually find in such cases, they were skittish about being handled. One of the ways we try to overcome that nervousness is by grooming. It not only improves the horses' coats, but also relaxes them and allows them to discover that our hands are gentle. Jenie and I brought these two new youngsters out to work on as we continued to chat.

The colts were distrustful of us at first, warily rolling their eyes. But clearly, being brushed was a luxury. As we curried their filthy, matted coats, their gaunt bodies soon began to relax. We oiled their dreadlocked manes and tails, and then Jenie and I began the tedious process of detangling the knotted hair. Our conversation floated from subject to subject as freely as the occasional puffy clouds drifting by overhead.

Jenie's brushing strokes grew longer as her colt's flaxen tail began to comb free. Finishing there, she switched back to a soft body brush. She was brushing the colt's rump and telling me about her family's plans for their annual trip when she allowed the brush to sweep down the colt's hind leg.

The startled colt lashed straight backward. His hoof nicked Jenie's extended arm one millisecond before it struck a bone-crushing blow to her face. Bright red blood gushed from her nose, spattering garishly on the dusty earth. Instinctively she staggered backward before collapsing.

Time stopped.

With dreamlike slowness Jenie fell to her knees, and I

saw her hand rise to her face—as if checking to see if it was still there. Blood covered her hand. It began trickling through her fingers. And down her wrist.

I couldn't get to her fast enough. A quick examination revealed no mobile fractures, not even any external damage other than a small cut on the side of her nose. Throughout the adrenaline-fueled frenzy of packing ice around her nose and trying to stop the bleeding, Jenie's only concern was for me. To soothe my anxious heart, she began to joke with me from under her face full of ice.

Several X rays later confirmed that Jenie had indeed sustained an immobile fracture of her nose. The damage was substantial enough for her to require a surgical rebreak and repairs to her shattered septum. She took it all in stride with easy grace. Judging by Jenie's level of concern, she had suffered nothing more serious than a stubbed toe.

I could never forget those initial, gut-twisting moments. The flashing movement of the colt's leg, the jolting sound of hoof crushing bone, the startling fall of Jenie's twisted body, and then the heart-stopping moments when I tried to reach her while my legs felt trapped in quicksand. All the possibilities of what could have happened jumbled in my brain, spiraling down to the same conclusion. One inch to the left and that smashing hoof would have struck her squarely in the temple.

My heart still writhes with the crushing knowledge that Jenie could have been killed. I agonized over what we were doing at Crystal Peaks. *Lord,* I prayed, *nothing on earth is worth risking the life of a child. Should I close the ranch?...*

June

It was the thirteenth of June, and at four o'clock in the afternoon the ranch was operating at full capacity. Half a dozen horse-and-rider teams were riding in the arena; several others were in various stages of tacking up or down. A three-year-old chestnut colt stood tied at a small hitching post near the bunkhouse lawn. We used this place for training young horses to relax and stand quietly amid commotion. And nowhere was there more commotion than around the bunkhouse, where we hosted a variety of activities for the kids.

The shady lawn in front is always filled with a cheerful clutter of white plastic chairs, each one artfully colored with permanent markers by our ranch kids. From here there are views of both the mountains and the arena, so it is a great place for visitors to relax and watch the children ride. This afternoon we had settled a disabled grandmother on the lawn in front of the hitching post. She always comes with her daughter and two granddaughters and seems to enjoy both the fresh air and the hubbub around her.

I had just stepped out of the arena to greet a young family on their first visit, feeling pleased that the father had come with his two daughters and their mother. It wasn't often we saw complete families at the ranch. I was talking with the little girls when it happened. Screaming pierced the air. It shot through my heart like a burning arrow.

I heard it before I saw the cause for the scream. The biggest dust devil I had ever seen was roaring inside the arena! Not one of my comforting, whimsical whirlwinds, this spinning devil was at least fifty feet across at the base, and already black with debris. Its gaping vortex devoured the sky. Before I realized my own movement, I was running toward the arena. The very air became solid matter as earth and sky converged. *Dear Jesus, the children!*

A sixty-gallon barrel came hurtling out of the sky and smashed into the arena gate, only steps away from me. I shielded my face as I struggled to see the kids through the chaos. Some were still mounted. Others had dismounted and were huddled in groups as their leaders tried to shield them from danger. One girl appeared to have tumbled off her horse and was ducking with her back to the wind. Quickly my brain ticked off the names and number of those in the arena, and all were accounted for.

The black monster spun out of the arena and toward the bunkhouse. The tied up chestnut colt was directly in its path. In the space of a heartbeat, the colt's alarm exploded into panic. Sheer terror turned this usually placid animal into a twisting blur of flailing hooves. In a desperate attempt to escape, he launched himself forward over the smooth bar of the hitching post. *Dear God!* I thought. *If his rope breaks...* Our disabled grandma was only a few feet away!

In an instant the white chairs were snatched away by the dust devil. The entire bunkhouse area was enshrouded in black, twisting debris. I strained to see the older woman, who was now completely engulfed in airborne material. *Lord, protect her,* I shouted inside my head.

Kelsie, one of our junior leaders, had been riding in the arena when the dust devil struck. Before she could move out of the way, it passed directly over her, lifting her from the saddle! My heart hammered like an emergency alarm as the chaos continued to swirl around me...

Three days later, after our team of five horses had competed in the premier endurance race in the Northwest, I began preparing our herd for the evening. Most of the finest horses in a five-state radius, including British Columbia, had competed. During that spectacular day my sweet unregistered, rescued mare, Ele, had won—by almost two miles! And Jenie, riding the tiniest of our Arabs in only the second race of the horse's career, came in second place.

When dusk descended, I had a quiet moment to reflect on all the gifts of that day. What a defining moment it had been for my precious horse. I sighed with deep satisfaction as evening color began to seep across the silent sky. The race camp was nestled in the foothills of the Cascade Range in a broad, grassy valley cradled by rugged, densely forested mountain flanks and rocky bluffs. The temperature fell with the setting sun, and streaks of sherbet orange and violet rose spread across the horizon until the sky itself seemed to be cheering in celebration of this triumphant day.

After blanketing our horses and settling them down for the night, I was desperately ready for bed myself. Even though my heart glowed with all of the richness of the day, my body felt awful. That morning I'd thought that I was coming down with the flu. The aching and fever had worsened during the race, and now I felt really nauseated, shivery, and exhausted. I longed to curl up in my warm sleeping bag for a few hours of restful oblivion.

I had just started to undress when I heard the sound of anxious hoof-beats. *Surely no one was riding now!* I pulled on a light fleece and ran out to investigate.

A horse from the ride camp was loose, trotting around our portable electric corral and whinnying frantically. In the dim light I could see a young man shadowing the renegade from a distance and hoped he would be able to catch his horse before there was trouble.

My little herd circled nervously as the strange horse grew more highly agitated. I slipped into the corral and was trying to take hold of my mare's halter when the unthinkable happened. The runaway suddenly wheeled and galloped through our corral, dragging the electrified line into all of my horses. Like a terrified flock of quail, they scattered up the steep slope behind the camp, snorting in terror, and thundered off into the wilderness.

Adrenaline seared through my body like an electric shock, and a silent scream exploded from my heart. *Dear Lord, help me!* My soul shattered as I watched my beloved horses stampede into the gaping jaws of imminent danger.

"Nancy, help!" I shouted over my shoulder to one of my leaders. I ran up the rough slope, but by the time I reached the crest not even dust lingered in the air. My precious family of horses was gone.

Twilight was falling fast into impenetrable darkness. I knew people who had lost their horses in the wilds. Some were found; some were not. Some had been injured so badly they had to be destroyed. Desperation gripped my heart.

I started praying.

The young man jogged up the slope behind me. I found out it wasn't his horse that was loose, but he willingly offered his help anyway. Together we began to run, following the fresh hoofprints as best we could in the gathering nightfall. In my illness and fear I was especially grateful for this Good Samaritan. Instead of returning to his warm bed at the campsite, he was out in the freezing, black wilderness searching after horses that weren't his—determined to accompany a sick woman that he didn't even know. He might have been flesh and blood, but to me he was an angel of mercy.

Together we followed the helter-skelter pattern of the panicked herd's tracks until darkness overtook us. We were both lightly dressed, not at all prepared to spend the night in the wilderness. The cold was beginning to penetrate what clothes we wore, and I knew we needed to get back to camp as quickly as we could. But without a moon we couldn't even see our feet, let alone tell where we'd come from.

At last we stumbled on a forgotten old logging road that seemed to lead back in the right direction. Stumbling down it, jogging blind, shaking with cold and fever, I began to wonder, *Why* my *horses? Why, out of the three hundred horses in the camp, was* my *corral singled out? Why were* my *horses driven off?* Alarm consumed me as completely as the darkness that surrounded me.

Minutes ticked into hours. Anxiety rolled over me like ocean waves, each one cresting with a new fear. *What if their blankets get caught on a branch or jagged rock? What if they plunge over a bluff? What if they find their way out on the other side of the mountains? What if someone finds them and decides to keep them?*

What if I never see them again?

I fought to keep the "what ifs" at bay and concentrated on what needed to be done.

Five and a half hours later we stumbled into camp.

My self-appointed guardian angel, satisfied that I was

safe, encouraged me to get some sleep. Instead, I hitched up a trailer and continued searching. Because it was the weekend of Father's Day, most of our team had gone home to be with their families. Only three of us remained in camp.

Nancy had located some logging roads leading more or less in the direction we thought the herd might have gone. We drove out and bumped and bounced over those roads for hours. Finally we were forced to turn around or risk getting stuck. After nail-biting minutes of tedious truck-and-trailer jockeying, we were finally able to bring both rigs around. I climbed out of the cab into the freezing darkness and began calling. I was certain that my mare would answer me as she always does at home, if she heard my voice. I called at intervals all the way back to camp.

It was early in the morning when Nancy and I collapsed into our sleeping bags. I had been on my feet for nearly twenty-four hours. My feverish body was crushed with exhaustion, but sleep wouldn't come. My troubled heart ached for my lost family. Ninety minutes later I quietly slipped out and began the search again.

I walked until a hint of gray began to illumine the frozen hills. The world lay completely still, and the air was as silent and empty as my soul. My horses were nowhere to be found.

I returned to the camp where one of the race organizers, hearing of my heartbreak, kindly offered to help me track down the horses. He fired up his ATV, and I slumped gratefully against his back as we bumped down the same roads that I had just covered in the dark.

Daylight revealed the hoofprints we had struggled to follow in the night. The horses had split up, so we abandoned the ATV and first tracked the three that had veered off into the forest. Their plunging flight had taken them up a mountainside so sheer that we had to haul ourselves up with protruding limbs and rocky outcrops. Everywhere we found freshly broken branches, churned-up soil, scrapes caused by iron shoes on stones—all marked the course of their terrified stampede. Near the top we saw where one of the horses had slipped and become high centered over fallen logs. Tufts of bloody horsehair and flesh were left on the rough bark and caught on twigs and stones—evidence of the horse's frantic struggle.

Eventually we came to a place where the trio had rested for a while before moving on. Up to that point, it was obvious they had been moving aimlessly—staggering up a high mountain flank and then zigzagging down the other side. Then, it appeared that they had sensed something to give them direction because their tracks suddenly converged and began to move purposefully due west.

We followed them to where the trail stopped. Hoofprints marked the ground in concentric circles as though the horses had been casting about like hounds for a scent. It was the exact spot where I had turned the truck around and had begun calling to them the night before. They must have recognized the familiar scent of my truck and trailer and followed it back. The marks of their hooves followed the tracks of my truck until they intersected the main race route, which led directly back to the camp.

The renegade and two of my horses had already arrived and were safely tied up. But Ele, the equine love of my life, and one more of our team were still missing. Once again, Nancy and I drove back to continue the search. Forrest, a tireless volunteer at the ranch, saddled up his little black mustang and began tracking from where the horses had first separated.

During my desperate hunt to find my mare's tracks, I began to fully understand the magnitude of the word "wilderness." My numbed mind tried and failed to push away the awful logic of the situation. They were highly trained endurance horses. By now they could have traveled fifty miles in *any* direction.

The combined effects of sleepless exhaustion and a persistent fever were slowly dimming the light in my head. My world began to spin. I grabbed at a tree branch as I fell to my knees. I blinked hard as if that would somehow clear my mind of the horrible conviction that was beginning to overwhelm my thoughts and my heart: It was likely that Ele would never be found.

I studied the earth in front of my knees, straining to focus on a single object—a rock, a pinecone—it didn't matter. I fought to stay conscious. Huddled on the forest floor, I prayed.

From somewhere below, the faint sound of Nancy's cell phone drifted through the trees. I could hear my friend calling for me, and I staggered back to my feet. I turned toward the direction of her muffled voice and willed my body to move forward...

JULY

From childhood, I have always been fascinated by violent weather. Thunderstorms especially intrigue me with their combination of sheer power and beauty. Like many avid hikers I have a backpack full of high-altitude, near-miss lightning stories; even so, a lightning storm still ranks high on my must-see list.

In our area, rising nearly four thousand feet beneath the shadow of the Cascades, thunderstorms can be particularly vicious. It's not uncommon for twenty-five hundred or more ground strikes to be recorded from a single storm cell. Many storms are accompanied by a violent rain that extinguishes most strike blazes before they get out of control. Nevertheless, wildfire in the Northwest is a fact of life.

One turbulent midsummer day, leaving my morning job at the fitness center in Bend, I ran to my truck through pelting rain. After diving into the cab, I pushed my hair back and could do nothing for a moment but watch. Winds howled through the ponderosa pines above me. Needles were driven to the ground in great windswept waves and then washed away in the mini flash flood. Water poured from the sky, splashing off the already standing water with the sound of riotous applause. It was as though all nature, every living thing, was shouting in joyful celebration.

I tried to comprehend the forces at work around me, this feast for my senses. I gazed and listened. I breathed in deeply the earthy wetness of the air. At last I started up the truck and made my way cautiously through the flooded streets toward the main road that led back to the ranch.

Soon the heavy gray skies gave way to deep purple as shafts of sunlight burst through the turbulent layers of clouds. Thunder crashed with deafening blows hard on the heels of each lightning flash, causing my shoulders to jump. The countryside rolled down and away before me, revealing a landscape laden with diamonds. The earth dazzled with reborn colors beneath the broken sky.

Suddenly in the distance an evil-looking coil of dark smoke caught my eye, writhing its way into the freshly cleansed sky. The belching, acrid cloud of black declared that this was no brush or timber fire. This was someone's home.

Even as I watched, the angry blaze unfurled like an ugly beast rising from sleep. My heart stopped, clenched with the cold hand of fear. This monster was growing in the approximate area of the ranch! *Dear God, the horses!*

I shoved the gas pedal to the floor...

AUGUST

Kids are masters at finding unique and creative ways to hurt themselves. In all families the law of averages holds true: the more kids, the more trips to the doctor. It's no different with equine families—as all horse owners are painfully aware. Since we have twenty-five four-legged "kids" at the ranch, we practically have ownership of a designated parking space at the Redmond Veterinary Clinic (RVC).

The RVC team has guided us from the very beginning, through dozens of crises and injuries, from stitching split lips and gashed legs to treating life-threatening colic, from ending a horse's suffering to assisting with newborn foals. These highly competent and compassionate professionals have soldiered on with us through all our ups and downs. Quick to laugh and unashamed to cry, they have become a cornerstone in our foundation of support at the ranch.

Our small pinto mare, Shelby, had come up severely lame, so I drove her into RVC for examination. Darrin, one of my dear veterinarian friends, watched with arms folded across his chest as I led Shelby around the yard at the clinic. He analyzed her gaits with the dark eyes of a predator measuring its prey.

Methodically, Darrin worked his way up from the simplest of tests—checking the mare's pressure points and joint flexion—to nerve blocking and finally X rays.

Each test yielded only limited information, and the sum of all still didn't point to a definitive diagnosis. Darrin carefully explained each X ray to me, pointing out clean, hard margins of bones, and the total lack of any sign of pathology. But he wasn't satisfied. Something was wrong. As he studied each film, he rubbed his chin with his thumb and forefinger, a gesture that by now I knew well.

After two hours of sleuthing, he followed an educated hunch and took one more X ray. I stroked Shelby's face as Darrin disappeared inside the clinic to develop the new film. It seemed only moments before he reappeared with a portable X-ray machine.

He wore a good poker face, but it was no match for a woman's intuition. "What is it?" I asked apprehensively. "What have you seen?"

"Probably nothing," he reassured me. He positioned the plates with the studied precision of a marksman focusing on the bull's-eye. I could tell he knew exactly what he was looking for. My heart shuddered.

I looked intently at the three latest X rays on the light bank but still saw nothing sinister. I glanced at Darrin. Grimly he pointed to each shadowy picture in turn. Squinting, I leaned toward the light. My heart sank. What had looked to me at first like a strand of dust on the film was actually a very fine black line. The last X ray showed it most clearly—a thin crack that ran from the back of Shelby's right front cannon bone more than halfway across the diameter.

"It's a hairline fracture," Darrin said. The words fell between us like stones. My mind crumbled under their weight. "Fracture" usually means death for a horse.

In his usual calming voice, Darrin explained that it was technically a "greenstick" fracture. In all of his years of practice he had never seen this type of injury on a pleasure horse. Except in racehorses, he confirmed, they're *extremely* rare.

The good news was that the area of intact bone was still supporting the leg. The bad news was that under even the slightest exertion the bone could shatter at any time.

Our only course of action was to wrap Shelby's leg for support and completely confine the mare. Horses carry about 70 percent of their weight on their front legs. In Shelby's case, with only one useable foreleg, simply loading and unloading her from the horse trailer became life threatening. The prognosis was guarded at best. Now there was little else we could do but submit to the dreaded regime of "watch and wait."

Only days later I was back at the clinic with another baffling condition. Blood was erupting from the left hind hoof of my Anglo-Arab mare Misha. Darrin saw me as he pushed through the clinic doors and shot me a commiserating smile. Within moments he had settled Misha's bleeding hoof firmly in his lap and, armed with a hoof knife, began to gently explore the mysterious hole that had appeared in the center of the mare's sole.

With his usual systematic precision, Darrin's diagnostic process ruled out one condition after another. His mental checklist neared the end, with still no answer in sight. Then his words came out one at a time—evidence of his deep concentration.

He had found granulation tissue inside the sole of the foot—a type of tissue commonly associated with wounds above the hoof. Granulation tissue is highly vascular and grows at an exponential rate. These qualities make it a vital resource in the healing process of soft tissue wounds.

But it was highly mysterious that this soft, bloody tissue should be found growing inside the sole of a hoof. The sole of a horse's hoof is made of keratin—the same material that forms human fingernails. It is a bloodless, hornlike structure that can withstand tremendous abuse. It was very unsettling to find blood coming from tissue that normally has no blood supply.

Finally, Darrin's diagnosis was narrowed down to one of two conditions: one was bad, the other worse. Either Misha had canker or cancer of the sole. Both were *extremely* rare conditions. *How strange,* I thought while contemplating what I had just heard the week before. *Now I have two horses with* extremely rare *conditions.*

SEPTEMBER

While September and October herald the coming of winter and blessed rest, they are in themselves exceptionally busy months. Between us, Troy and I hold down six jobs, and they all seem to converge in the fall—an enormous weight riding on the back of an already exhausting summer workload.

Troy's landscaping business requires long hours of

hard physical labor. Then, when he comes home at night, he switches to his role as administrator of Crystal Peaks—probably the least enjoyable task on the ranch. Handling all the paperwork associated with running an enormous nonprofit organization is nearly a full-time job in itself. Finally, he is a professional videographer, shoehorning his studio time in from late evening to the small hours of the morning. Like many self-employed people, he balances a superhuman schedule to make ends meet.

In the mornings I divide my time between two health clubs in neighboring towns. I work as a personal trainer at the Athletic Club of Bend, and at the Athletic Club of Sisters I instruct a difficult workout class—affectionately dubbed "Boot Camp" by participants. Afterward, from noon until dark, I have the privilege of being the director of our ranch. Even though my schedule is demanding, I feel blessed to have jobs that I love so much. But between Troy's work and mine, we see little of each other from April to October. We try hard to set aside "oasis" times for ourselves and each other, but the reality of running two businesses and the ranch programs from our home can be crushing.

Sometimes a brief oasis can be found in just riding together in the cab of our truck. That was the case one perfect September evening, warm and still. We had just finished hauling hay at the end of one of our "Atlas-imitation" days and sat in near silence as the truck chugged up the last hill toward our house. We were exhausted down to our very souls.

Troy pulled up in front of the garage. He turned the ignition key off—and just sat there, staring straight ahead, unmoving. His stonelike profile was etched with fatigue and grit from the day's work.

I didn't feel much like moving either. The momentary rest felt like cool water on my sweaty face.

I looked again at Troy and suddenly realized that this was no ordinary rest. His face was hollow and drawn as if in tremendous pain.

"Troy? What's wrong?" My words tripped out and sprawled uselessly before him. I could see as well as feel him withdraw to some place inside himself. His eyes were glassed over with exhaustion. My stomach twisted as I waited for him to speak.

He looked down. Tears streaked down his brown cheeks. Although deeply tenderhearted, Troy was always so strong. Fear gripped my throat.

"Today," he began, his words coming out with agonizing slowness, "it took all of my willpower *not* to go to the bank and empty my accounts...and just leave." His voice trailed off to a whisper as he dropped his face into his hands. "It's too much for me, Kim. I can't do this anymore..."

Such was the previous season of my life. I learned so much about what it really means to run the hurdles of life. Challenges rose on nearly every front—and with them heavy doses of fear.

In a single season we faced financial ruin and could have lost the ranch. One of the Lord's precious lambs—our new young leader, Jenie—might easily have been killed. We were struck by a minitornado that tore through an arena full of kids. Several of my horse family—including my equine soul mate—were scattered and lost in the wilderness of the Cascade Mountains. Everything we have worked so hard to create could have burned to the ground from a single lightning strike. Two of my angels in horsehair were stricken with rare—almost unknown—conditions. And the love of my life, my best friend, my husband—the pillar who supports my heart—nearly collapsed.

My home, my ranch, my family, friends, children, horses, and husband—all faced destruction. All the beams of strength in my life were attacked. I was challenged down to the very foundations of my faith. And the questions came, aimed like flaming arrows at my soul. *If God is so good, why did He let all of this happen to you? If He loves you so much, why did He hurt you so deeply? If God is really in control, why is your life so out of control?* Like hissing darts they rained down on my spirit, a volley launched to destroy my faith, my love, my peace, my joy.

Hope, shining like a beacon, can be an easy target for such evil missiles—when it is founded solely on human strength. But true hope has its foundation buried deep within the solid Rock of Jesus Christ. I stood through that season—and I continue to stand—not by any strength that I possess in myself, but only by the strength that has been given to me by a faithful God.

I am not a powerful woman, but I believe in a powerful God. Instead of cowering under the hail of fiery lies, I lifted my sword of truth, the Word of God, and began to fight back. Every arrow, shot with the intention of maiming and destroying, shattered into flaming pieces around my feet.

Like a lighthouse guiding those who are lost, true hope shines on, and even the blackest darkness cannot overcome the power of its light. Even death itself cannot overcome hope. When it is built on the Rock, it will stand.

Even my own death cannot separate me from hope. Because of that truth, my heart has risen from being a victim to becoming a victor.

Yes, financially speaking, we could have lost the ranch. We could have—but we didn't. Because God is faithful. The finances came when we needed them the most.

Yes, Jenie could have been killed right before my eyes. No endeavor—no matter how lovingly motivated—is worth risking the life of a child. There has never been a time when I felt more pressure to close the ranch. But truth fought back! Risk exists in *all* the things we do. Our fear of the "what ifs" must never drive us backward into complacency or paralysis. Or allow us to forget God's faithfulness.

Jenie's nose was broken—but not her faith in Christ. She went on to share her faith inside the quiet walls of a surgeon's office when her doctor momentarily stepped from behind the cool curtain of professionalism to become a seeker who simply needed to hear the truth. Today, the beauty of Jenie's reconstructed nose is one step closer to matching the incredible inner beauty that radiates from her heart.

Yes, children, leaders, adults, visitors, and horses could all have been hurt by the massive dust devil that tore through our arena. But Kelsie, with her usual amazing presence of mind, threw her arms around her horse's neck as the twister sucked her from the saddle. Hanging on tightly, she kicked her horse into a leaping gallop, and they escaped unharmed.

At random chairs began dropping from the sky. But no one was hit. The colt righted himself without damage. And Grandma, with the wisdom of those who have lived a lot of life, took it all in stride. A hasty accounting revealed that everyone had emerged from the remarkable ordeal unscathed. Everyone there was a witness to God's faithfulness.

I had pushed my hair back and replaced my hat and then made my way down to the family I'd left by the tack room. They were huddled together, pale and wide-eyed. With a ragged, exaggerated smile, I said, "So! Where were we?"

Yes, my horses were scattered into the wilderness. They could have been hurt or killed in any number of ways. But by God's faithfulness, they were not. Miraculously the last two missing ones—including my beloved Ele—were found many miles away, having navigated certain equine disaster without a single scratch. More arrows, more lies, fell to the ground in smoldering pieces.

Yes, our property—and everything built upon it—could have been destroyed by fire. Our ranch *was* struck by lightning—twice! An astonished Forrest, one of our ranch volunteers, recounted actually seeing a jagged bolt hit the ground in the main horse paddock. A fraction of an instant later, a second bolt smashed into the corner of our hay barn. But God is faithful. Even though the corner support beam of the barn was blown into bits and nearly all the ranch electrical systems were destroyed, *nothing* burned. Nothing except another lie turning to charred embers at my feet.

Yes, our horses were struck with rare and potentially lethal conditions. Once again, I raised my sword of faith and hope. Did they die? No! Because God is faithful. They both have fully recovered and continue to live their lives as gentle servants and friends of our ranch kids.

Yes, the man of my dreams, the love of all my days, buckled under the pressure of our chosen life. He could have left; he could have fled the titanic waves of stress that currently roll through his life.

But he didn't...because God is faithful. The Lord heard the humble pleas of a simple woman who prays for her husband every day. Hand in hand, shoulder to shoulder, and heart to heart, Troy and I have reestablished ourselves. Today we are a stronger force together than we ever were before.

All of these flaming arrows that were launched to destroy have only added fuel to the fire that burns in my heart—because I know that faith grows only when it's forced to. I stand on the knowledge that God is *faithful*. Supported by that fact, I kick at the smoldering embers that have fallen at my feet. Pitiful little sparks scatter into the air, flaring weakly before disintegrating into wisps of nothing more than smoke. With my hands and my breath I blow the ashes away and smooth off the rock of truth on which I stand.

Such was this last season.

So, once again I stand up to all of the hurdles on the track of life. I eye them from a distance as I warm up for another season. For I have learned something vital from this last stretch of time and those before it. It's not as important that I clear the hurdles in perfect form as it is that I just keep running.

Throughout the race there are times when the hardships of life weigh on every side, drawing and dividing faith and strength. It is hard to focus on the task at hand, even harder to see the finish. Entangled steps weave and falter in a desperate attempt for endurance—and answers.

There is an answer.

Therefore, since we are surrounded by such a huge crowd of witnesses to the life of faith, let us strip off every weight that slows us down, especially the sin that so easily hinders our progress. And let us run with endurance the race that God has set before us. We do this by keeping our eyes on Jesus, on whom our faith depends from start to finish.

HEBREWS 12:1–2

The real tragedy would be to stop in the middle of the race. A momentary inspection of wounds is one thing, but to give up in the middle of life is another. For those who will simply commit to running the race, putting one foot in front of the other, no matter how big or small the step—for those, in the end, the victory will come.

Because God is faithful.

The Choice

So MUCH OF our life seems to just happen. We have all shared moments of throwing our hands in the air in utter dismay of a raucous day's offerings. Yet in reality, most of our life is what we *choose* for it to be. As violently as external forces push, we are still the master of our own will.

Difficulties, hurdles, hardships, whatever name we know them by, one thing is certain—they visit us all. No life is immune from suffering. As certain as we breathe, we *will* know pain. It is a shapeless void that shifts into as many faces as humanity itself. It has no sense of justice or timing. Like a wall of fire, pain rises where it chooses, consuming whatever it can. It is a famine that gnaws at the soul.

Mounting like impenetrable black fog, pain envelops everything—light, love, hope. It is a dark chasm of loneliness. It is a precipice of despair. It is a wailing child collapsed in a barren orchard.

The view from within this lifeless place is the same in any direction—it is all ash. It wraps around us like a black desolate ring encircling our impoverished soul. There is nowhere to run, nowhere to hide. It becomes the truest definition of being surrounded.

When our hope falls to its knees and takes its last gasp before death, there is an answer. It is simple. It lies free for every soul to choose. When you are surrounded, instead of anxiously looking from side to side, look up. Change your view with a new perspective.

Look up and see what the Maker sees. Instead of a destroyed circle, He sees a vital clearing where the light of truth can penetrate. Instead of a ring of ash, He sees previous snaring distractions burned into usable nutrients. Instead of barrenness, He sees a circle where something enduring can grow, something that is beautiful, something that is permanent.

God doesn't see wild flames on every side lapping at our souls. He sees cleansing fire that consumes the dross of complacency. He sees hearts tempered with strength, purified like gold.

God doesn't see a descending black fog encircling its shrouded victims with the icy grip of despair. He sees a temporary veil that encourages faith to rise out of meandering convenience and be galvanized with power into a force that moves mountains.

God doesn't see a hungry precipice yawning open to swallow us whole. He sees the perfect opportunity for hope to unfurl its wings and soar free over logic that tells us what is and isn't possible.

Even the utter devastation of death's finality before God is not final. It is His desire that our loss will embolden and motivate us to love those who remain with even greater passion and selflessness.

God didn't see a ring of cottony, fallen hair surrounding a horse near death. He saw a golden halo circling like a wedding band the very hearts on which His miraculous love was soon to fall.

When we feel like we're surrounded, it is only because we truly are—we are surrounded by His love.

It is true, the pain that we feel in this life is certain. What is equally certain is how we choose to feel about the pain. It can destroy us—or define us.

Like standing on a mountainous trail, we can *choose* which way to go. We can *choose* where we end up. When confronted by pain, we can *choose* to take the descending trail that most often leads to a dark and lonely place, pitted with mires of helplessness, hopelessness, despair.

Or we can select the ascending trail and, with some effort and perseverance, we can *choose* to allow our pain to motivate us toward becoming better people, to move us toward a better place. A place where love transcends selfishness, where faith bulldozes the "what ifs," and where peace enfolds the heart like a warm blanket. It is a place where joy takes on as many faces as humanity. It is a place where flowers bloom in ash.

Like an unstoppable wave of light pouring over the horizon, it is a place where hope rises.

Hope Continues

Because of our united compassion for the children and horses in this book, it is only our nature to wonder, "Where are they now?" It is my deepest joy to share in the victories of "my family."

"The Beginning"
Jessica's broken family has found complete healing in the love of the Lord. Jessica herself has risen into a beautiful, accomplished college graduate who is now yielding her life to the children of Peru where she is working as a teacher.

"The Wishing Tree"
Heather and Breanna, who escaped their abusive father with their mother, Diane, have seen their dreams become a reality. They now share a life of freedom in the country with three horses of their own.

"Chosen One"
Maci's injuries were serious; she not only sustained a skull fracture and lacerations to her head and face, she also severed the main nerve branch that controls facial movement above the eyes. Thankfully, by the grace of God, the nerve has completely regenerated and all the wonderful expressions of a little girl have returned to Maci's face.

"Run Through Fire"
Sarah continues to work at the ranch and endurance race Mighty Mojave. She is currently enrolled in college to become an equine veterinary technician.

"It's Good"

Jamie, the little girl that doctors thought would not survive, is now walking and riding without assistance. She is currently learning sign language and is still one of the happiest kids I know.

"Lord, Have Mercy"

Mercy, the pregnant mare that died, did not do so in vain. Since then, we have rescued another horse from the same property. He is one of the rarest horses that I have ever known. Not only is his coloration rare—a palomino Arabian—he is also exceptionally special because he is the only horse I'm aware of to have survived being hit by a semi truck and trailer! He has completely stolen my heart, and due to his pale golden color and extraordinary survival, I have appropriately named him "Halo."

"A Perfect Match"

Mary still lives in Washington State with her husband and children. She continues to be an inspiration to all who meet her.

"Solemn Vow"

Solemn, the severely starved black mare, gained three hundred pounds...and then some. To our enormous surprise, we discovered that she was already pregnant when she came to the ranch. She delivered a completely healthy foal nine months after her rescue! "Solemn's Blessing" was born April 24. She is a chocolate-colored bay with four white socks and a wide blaze. Blessing, giving some of the best kisses on the ranch, is rapidly growing into every child's dream horse.

"Miracle"

Jennifer continues to soar with confidence. She is now part of a strong youth group and is also a member of her high-school equestrian team. She has gone on to live her dream and show Miracle with success.

Supporting Hope

All programs and services offered by Crystal Peaks Youth Ranch are free of charge. Nearly all the children who come to the ranch are from deeply challenging circumstances. Charges of any kind would prevent most from being able to use the ranch. Crystal Peaks Youth Ranch, therefore, is supported by individual financial gifts, grants, and fund-raising events.

It takes many strong stones to build a strong foundation. If you would like to become part of this team of dedicated supporters, please contact us by e-mail at Crypkranch@aol.com or write us at the address below. Your interest in the lives of these children and their families will have a lasting impact and is deeply appreciated.

Thank you.

Crystal Peaks Youth Ranch
19344 Innes Market Road
Bend, OR 97701

About the Author

One of Kim Meeder's first riding experiences came at the age of nine, on the day of her parents' funeral. Riding quickly became a healing refuge for her after the shock of their murder-suicide. By the love of a little mare and a merciful God, the young girl's life was saved.

This saving grace was a portent of what was to come, years later, when Kim and her husband, Troy, made the decision to transform a former rock quarry into a small ranch. In 1996, Crystal Peaks Youth Ranch (CPYR) was born. CPYR is a unique nonprofit organization that rescues abused and neglected horses and pairs them with seeking children. The ranch's program pairs one child with one horse, guided by one leader, 100 percent of the time. All this is done free of charge.

The ranch supports twenty-five horses and meets the needs of four to five thousand visitors every year. CPYR works closely with nearly every organization that deals with youth and families. Although the ranch activities are designed for youth at risk, all children of all ages are welcome.

A portion of the proceeds from the sale of this book goes to support the work of Crystal Peaks.

Kim Meeder is an accomplished athlete, having competed on a national level in Nordic ski racing and participated in the Olympic biathlon trials. She has also set two world records in power lifting and is an avid surfer. As a fledgling mountaineer, Kim has climbed many of the highest peaks in Oregon, Washington, and California.